PRAISE FOR *TEN GLOBAL TRENDS EVERY SMART PERSON SHOULD KNOW*

"Read this book and find out why, if you are not an optimist, you should be."

—**Vernon L. Smith**, Nobel Prize–winning economist and George L. Argyros Endowed Chair in Finance and Economics, Chapman University

"If you learn about the world through daily news and social media, you have probably missed the greatest stories of our time. But don't worry, you'll quickly catch up with this tour de force. It will make you smarter—and happier. I am a card-carrying optimist, but Ronald Bailey and Marian Tupy manage to make even me more hopeful about humanity."

—**Johan Norberg**, author of *Progress: Ten Reasons to Look Forward to the Future*, named by *The Economist* as one of the best books of 2016

"This is an astonishing collection of positive trends. I want every young person to see it and begin to escape the indoctrination in pessimism they have been subjected to by the media and the education system. Making the world a much better place is clearly possible."

—**Matt Ridley**, author of *The Rational Optimist: How Prosperity Evolves* and *How Innovation Works: And Why It Flourishes in Freedom*

TEN GLOBAL TRENDS

EVERY SMART PERSON SHOULD KNOW

AND MANY OTHERS YOU WILL FIND INTERESTING

RONALD BAILEY AND MARIAN L. TUPY

CATO
INSTITUTE

ISBN: 978-1-948647-73-1
eISBN: 978-1-948647-74-8

Publisher's Cataloging-in-Publication Data

Names: Bailey, Ronald, author. | Tupy, Marian L., author.
Title: Ten global trends every smart person should know , and many others you will find interesting / Ronald Bailey and Marian L. Tupy.
Description: Includes bibliographical references. | Washington, D.C. : Cato Institute, 2020.
Identifiers: LCCN 2020939606 | ISBN 978-1-948647-73-1 (Hardcover) | 978-1-948647-74-8 (ebook)
Subjects: LCSH Globalization. | World health. | Environmental policy--International cooperation. | Environmental management. | Climatic changes--21st century. | International relations. | International economic relations. | Economic development. | Natural resources. | World politics--21st century.
Classification: LCC JZ1318 .B35 2020 | DDC 303.48/2--dc23

Jacket design: FaceOut Studio, Molly Von Borstel.
Cover imagery: Shutterstock.
Book and graphics design: Luis Ahumada Abrigo and Guillermina Sutter Schneider.

Printed in Canada.

Cato Institute
1000 Massachusetts Avenue NW
Washington, DC 20001
www.cato.org

To Steve and Leslie Frantz, and Stuart and Brock Lending, the travel buddies who have journeyed so far with me, both in body and intellect. And to my dearest Pamela.

Ronald Bailey

In memory of my loving grandmother Maria Lapinova, who survived Nazism and communism and was always grateful for the little things in life. She taught me proper perspective.

Marian L. Tupy

CONTE

I see all this progress, and it fills me with conviction and hope
that further progress is possible. This is not optimistic.
It is having a clear and reasonable idea about how things are.
It is having a worldview that is constructive and useful.

Hans Rosling, *Factfulness: Ten Reasons We're Wrong about the World—and Why Things Are Better Than You Think*

INTRODUCTION
WHY THIS BOOK?

You can't fix what is wrong in the world if you don't know what's actually happening. In this book, straightforward charts and graphs, combined with succinct explanations, will provide you with easily understandable access to the facts that busy people need to know about how the world is really faring.

Polls show that most smart people tend to believe that the state of the world is getting worse rather than better. Consider a 2016 survey by the global public opinion company YouGov that asked folks in 17 countries, "All things considered, do you think the world is getting better or worse, or neither getting better nor worse?"[1] Fifty-eight percent of respondents thought that the world is getting worse, and 30 percent said that it is doing neither. Only 11 percent thought that things are getting better. In the United States, 65 percent of Americans thought

that the world is getting worse, and 23 percent said neither. Only 6 percent of Americans responded that the world is getting better.

This dark view of the prospects for humanity and the natural world is, in large part, badly mistaken. We demonstrate it in these pages using uncontroversial data taken from official and scientific sources.

Of course, some global trends are negative. As Harvard University psychologist Steven Pinker says: "It's essential to realize that progress does not mean that everything gets better for everyone, everywhere, all the time. That would be a miracle, that wouldn't be progress."[2] For example, manmade climate change arising largely from increasing atmospheric concentrations of carbon dioxide released from burning fossil fuels could become a significant problem

for humanity during this century. The spread of plastic marine debris is a big and growing concern. Many wildlife populations are declining, and tropical forest area continues shrinking. In addition, far too many people are still malnourished and dying in civil and sectarian conflicts around the globe. And, of course, the world is afflicted by the current coronavirus pandemic.

However, many of the global trends we describe are already helping redress such problems. For example, the falling price of renewable energy sources incentivizes the switch away from fossil fuels. Moreover, increasingly abundant agriculture is globally reducing the percentage of people who are hungry while simultaneously freeing up land so that forests are now expanding in much of the world. And unprecedentedly rapid research has significantly advanced testing, tracking, and treatment technologies to ameliorate the coronavirus contagion.

PSYCHOLOGICAL GLITCHES MISLEAD YOU

So why do so many smart people wrongly believe that, all things considered, the world is getting worse?

Way back in 1965, Johan Galtung and Mari Holmboe Ruge, from the Peace Research Institute Oslo, observed, "There is a basic asymmetry in life between the positive, which is difficult and takes time, and the negative, which is much easier and takes less time—compare the amount of time needed to bring up and socialize an adult person and the amount of time needed to kill him in an accident, the amount of time needed to build a house and to destroy it in a fire, to make an airplane and to crash it, and so on."[3] News is bad news; steady progress is not news.

Smart people especially seek to be well informed and so tend to be voracious consumers of news. Since journalism focuses on dramatic things and events that go wrong, the nature of news thus tends to mislead readers and viewers into thinking that the world is in worse shape than it really is. This mental shortcut causes many of us to confuse what comes easily to mind with what is true; it was first identified in 1973 by behavioral scientists Amos Tversky and Daniel Kahneman as the "availability bias."[4] Another reason for the ubiquity of mistaken gloom derives from a quirk of our evolutionary psychology. A Stone Age man hears a rustle in the grass. Is it the wind or a lion? If he assumes it's the wind and the rustling turns out to be a lion, then he's not an ancestor. We are the descendants of the worried folks who tended to assume that all rustles in the grass were dangerous predators and not the wind. Because of this instinctive negativity bias, most of us attend far more to bad rather than to good news. The upshot is that we are again often misled into thinking that the world is worse than it is.

"Judgment creep" is yet another explanation for the prevalence of wrong-headed pessimism. We are misled about the state of the world because we have a tendency to continually raise our threshold for success as we make progress, argue Harvard University psychologist Daniel Gilbert and his colleagues. "When problems become rare, we count more things as problems. Our studies suggest that when the world gets better, we become harsher critics of it, and this can cause us to mistakenly conclude that it hasn't actually gotten better at all," explains Gilbert. "Progress, it seems, tends to mask itself."[5] Social, economic, and environmental problems are being judged intractable because reductions in their prevalence lead people to see more of them. More than 150 years ago, political scientist Alexis de Tocqueville noted a similar phenomenon as societies progress, one that has since been called the Tocqueville effect.

What, though, accounts for progress?

Some smart folk who acknowledge that considerable social, economic, and environmental progress has been made still worry that progress will not necessarily continue.

"Human beings still have the capacity to mess it all up. And it may be that our capacity to mess it up is growing," asserted Cambridge University political scientist David Runciman in a July 2017 *Guardian* article. He added: "For people to feel deeply uneasy about the world we inhabit now, despite all these indicators pointing up, seems to me reasonable, given the relative instability of the evidence of this progress, and the [unpredictability] that overhangs it. Everything really is pretty fragile."[6]

Runciman is not alone. The worry that civilization is just about to go over the edge of a precipice has a long history. After all, many earlier civilizations and regimes have collapsed, including the Babylonian, Roman, Tang, and Mayan Empires, and more recently the Ottoman and Soviet Empires.

In their 2012 book, *Why Nations Fail: The Origins of Power, Prosperity, and Poverty*, economists Daron Acemoglu and James Robinson persuasively outline reasons for the exponential improvement in human well-being that started about two centuries ago.

They begin by arguing that since the Neolithic agricultural revolution, most societies have been organized around "extractive" institutions—political and economic systems that funnel resources from the masses to the elites.[7]

In the 18th century, some countries—including Britain and many of its colonies—shifted from extractive to inclusive institutions. "Inclusive economic institutions that enforce property rights, create a level playing field, and encourage investments in new technologies and skills are more conducive to economic growth than extractive economic institutions that are structured to extract resources from the many by the few," they write. "Inclusive economic institutions are in turn supported by, and support, inclusive political institutions," which "distribute political power widely in a pluralistic manner and are able to achieve some amount of political centralization so as to establish law and order, the foundations of secure property rights, and an inclusive market economy."[8] Inclusive institutions are similar to one another in their respect for individual liberty. They include democratic politics, strong private property rights, the rule of law, enforcement of contracts, freedom of movement, and a free press. Inclusive institutions are the bases of the technological and entrepreneurial innovations that produced a historically unprecedented rise in living standards in those countries that embraced them, including the United States, Japan, and Australia as well as the countries in Western Europe. They are qualitatively different from the extractive institutions that preceded them.

The spread of inclusive institutions to more and more countries was uneven and occasionally reversed. Those advances—and in University of Illinois at Chicago economist Deirdre McCloskey's view, the key role played by major ideological shifts—resulted in what

McCloskey calls the "great enrichment," which boosted average incomes thirtyfold to a hundredfold in those countries where they have taken hold.

The examples of societal disintegration cited earlier, whether Roman, Tang, or Soviet, occurred in extractive regimes. Despite crises such as the Great Depression, there are no examples so far of countries with long-established inclusive political and economic institutions suffering similar collapses.

In addition, confrontations between extractive and inclusive regimes, such as World War II and the Cold War, have generally been won by the latter. That suggests that liberal free-market democracies are resilient in ways that enable them to forestall or rise above the kinds of shocks that destroy brittle extractive regimes.

If inclusive liberal institutions can continue to be strengthened and further spread across the globe, the auspicious trends documented in this book will extend their advance, and those that are currently negative will turn positive. By acting through inclusive institutions to increase knowledge and pursue technological progress, past generations met their needs and hugely increased the ability of our generation to meet our needs. We should do no less for our own future generations. That is what sustainable development looks like.

TOP 10 TRENDS

THE GREAT ENRICHMENT

Since 1820, the size of the world's economy has grown more than a hundredfold. Over the past 200 years, the world population grew somewhat less than eightfold. Measuring the size of the economy over time is challenging, however. One commonly used measure is the 2011 constant international dollar, which is a hypothetical unit of currency that has the same purchasing power parity value that the U.S. dollar had in the United States at a given point in time. Economic growth figures are adjusted to reflect the local prices of products to give a better idea of the purchasing power of individuals in different countries over time.

Between 1500 and 1820, world gross product grew about 0.3 percent per year, eventually tripling from $430 billion to $1.2 trillion.[9] As some countries began adopting freer markets and the rule of law spread along with increased international trade, the pace of global economic growth sped up to 1.3 percent annually, increasing the size of the world economy to $3.4 trillion in 1900. Since that time, global economic growth has averaged slightly more than 3 percent per year, boosting world gross product to more than $121 trillion by 2018.[10]

What about the future? The Intergovernmental Panel on Climate Change's (IPCC) benchmark middle-of-the-road scenario—which features medium levels of economic and population growth—projects that the global economy will grow to about $600 trillion by 2100.[11] The IPCC expects that the global economic growth rate will average about 2 percent annually in that scenario. If, however, global economic growth were to maintain its 2.8 percent average rate since 2000, the world's economy would instead increase by almost tenfold to $1.1 quadrillion by 2100.[12]

> "Since 1820, the size of the world's economy has grown more than a hundredfold. Over the past 200 years, the world population grew somewhat less than eightfold."

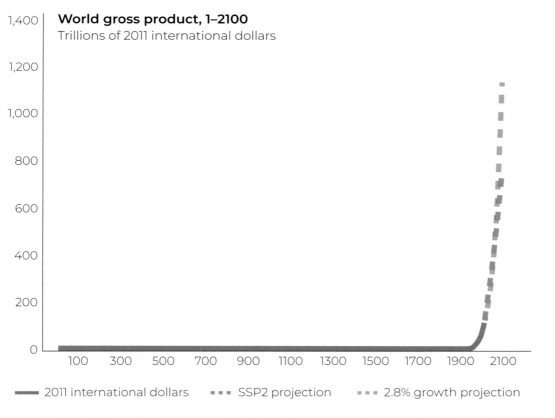

World gross product, 1–2100
Trillions of 2011 international dollars

Legend:
- 2011 international dollars
- SSP2 projection
- 2.8% growth projection

Sources: Angus Maddison Project Database 2010 and 2018; World Bank, "Global Gross Domestic Product, Purchasing Power Parity" chart.
Note: SSP2 = Shared Socioeconomic Pathway scenario 2

THE END OF POVERTY

The vast majority of our ancestors lived and died in humanity's natural state of disease-ridden abject poverty and pervasive ignorance. University of Paris economists François Bourguignon and Christian Morrisson estimate that as late as 1820, nearly 84 percent of the world's population lived in extreme poverty (roughly on less than $1.90 per day per person).[13] That was when political and economic liberalization in some parts of the world kicked off what economist Deirdre McCloskey calls "the great enrichment." Consequently, the global proportion of people living in extreme poverty began slowly declining to 66 percent in 1910 and 55 percent by 1950. According to the World Bank, 42 percent of the globe's population was still living in absolute poverty in 1981. In other words, it took 160 years for the rate of extreme poverty to fall by half. Fortunately, the pace of global poverty reduction has greatly sped up.[14] The latest World Bank assessment reckons that the share of the world's inhabitants living in extreme poverty

> "The latest World Bank assessment reckons that the share of the world's inhabitants living in extreme poverty fell to 8.6 percent in 2018."

fell to 8.6 percent in 2018. In 1990, about 1.9 billion of the world's people lived in extreme poverty;[15] by 2018, that number had dropped to 650 million, even despite ongoing population increases that put the world population at 7.5 billion.

Maintaining the current rate of poverty reduction would result in less than 5 percent of the world's population living in destitution in 2030. And in 2015, the United Nations set the goal of eradicating extreme poverty by 2030 for all people everywhere. It might even be attainable.

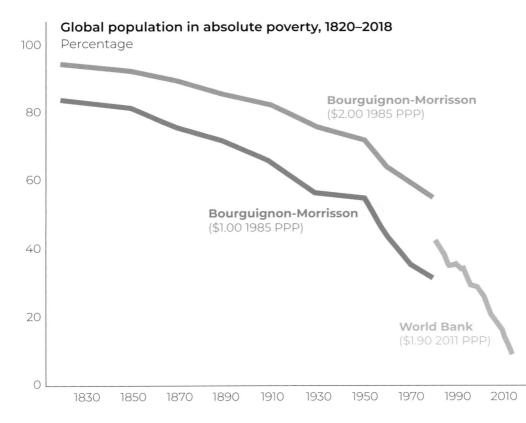

Global population in absolute poverty, 1820–2018
Percentage

Bourguignon-Morrisson
($2.00 1985 PPP)

Bourguignon-Morrisson
($1.00 1985 PPP)

World Bank
($1.90 2011 PPP)

Sources: World Bank, "Poverty Headcount Ratio" chart; François Bourguignon and Christian Morrisson, "Inequality among World Citizens: 1820–1992," *American Economic Review* 92, no. 4 (2002): 727–744.

Note: PPP = purchasing power parity

ARE WE RUNNING OUT OF RESOURCES?

In his 1968 book *The Population Bomb*, Stanford University biologist Paul Ehrlich warned that overpopulation and overconsumption would result in the exhaustion of resources and a global catastrophe.[16] To understand whether that is likely to happen, it is important to recognize that resources are not finite in the same way that a slice of pizza is finite. That's because the totality of our resources is neither known nor fixed.

In a competitive economy, humanity's knowledge about the value and availability of something tends to be reflected in its price. If prices fall, resources can be deemed to have become more abundant relative to demand. If prices increase, they can be deemed to have become less abundant, again relative to demand. Higher prices also create incentives for innovation, including discoveries of new deposits, greater efficiency of use, and the development of substitutes.

In a recent paper, one of us looked at prices for 50 foundational commodities covering energy, food, materials, and metals. The data were collected by the World Bank and the International Monetary Fund between 1980 and 2017. The paper found that the nominal prices of 9 commodities fell, whereas the nominal prices of 41 commodities increased. The average nominal price of 50 commodities rose by 62.7 percent. Adjusted for inflation,

> "Humanity has not yet run out of a single supposedly nonrenewable resource. In fact, resources tend to become more abundant over time relative to the demand for them."

however, 43 commodities declined in price, 2 remained equally valuable, and only 5 commodities increased in price. On average, the real price of 50 commodities fell by 36.3 percent.[17]

Between 1980 and 2017, the inflation-adjusted global hourly income per person also grew by 80.1 percent. Therefore, for the amount of work required, commodities became 64.7 percent cheaper. Put differently, commodities that took 60 minutes of work to buy in 1980 took only 21 minutes of work to buy in 2017.[18] All in all, resources are not being depleted in the way that Ehrlich feared they would—as witnessed by the fact that humanity has not yet run out of a single supposedly nonrenewable resource. In fact, resources tend to become more abundant over time relative to the demand for them.

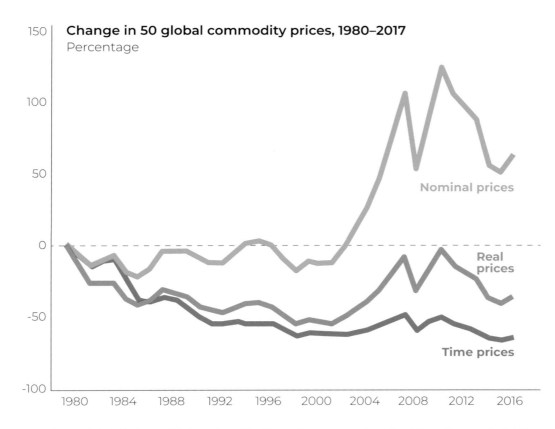

Change in 50 global commodity prices, 1980–2017
Percentage

Nominal prices

Real prices

Time prices

Source: Gale L. Pooley and Marian L. Tupy, "The Simon Abundance Index: A New Way to Measure Availability of Resources," Cato Policy Analysis no. 857, December 4, 2018.

TREND 4

PEAK POPULATION

World population will likely peak at 9.8 billion people at around 2080 and fall to 9.5 billion by 2100 in the medium-fertility scenario calculated by demographer Wolfgang Lutz and his colleagues at the International Institute for Applied Systems Analysis.[19] Alternatively, assuming rapid economic growth, technological advancement, and rising levels of educational attainment for both sexes—all factors that tend to lower fertility—Lutz projects

> "Instead of having many children in the hope that a few might survive, more parents around the world now aim at providing those few whom they do have with the skills and social capital that will enable them to flourish in a modern economy."

that world population will more likely peak at about 8.9 billion by 2060 and decline to 7.8 billion by the end of the 21st century.[20] Today, global population stands at about 7.7 billion.

These projections contrast with the United Nations' median population projection, which reckons that there is a good chance that the world population will peak at 10.9 billion before 2100.[21] Lutz and his fellow researchers point out that past UN projections have been too high. That has been the case, they argue, because the UN does not take adequate account of the effects on fertility of increased levels of education, especially the schooling of girls and women.

Other global trends—such as steeply falling child mortality rates, increased urbanization, rising incomes, and the spread of political and economic freedom—all strongly correlate with families' choosing to have fewer children. Instead of having many children in the hope that a few might survive, more parents around the world now aim at providing those few whom they do have with the skills and social capital that will enable them to flourish in a modern economy. The trend toward lower population growth is good news because it means that the global expansion of reproductive freedom is empowering more families to decide how many children they wish to have.

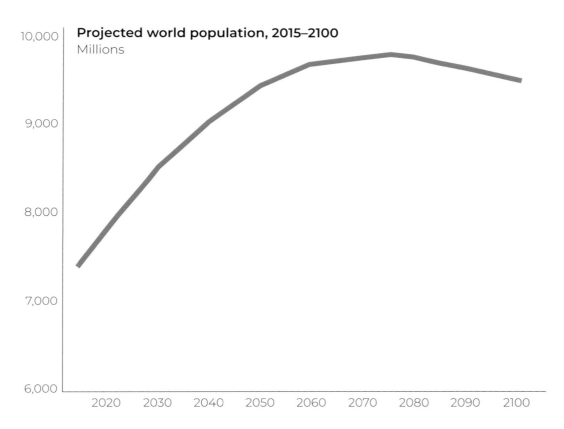

Projected world population, 2015–2100
Millions

Sources: Wolfgang Lutz et al., eds., "Demographic and Human Capital Scenarios for the 21st Century: 2018 Assessment for 201 Countries," European Commission Joint Research Centre, 2018, p. 8; UN Department of Economic and Social Affairs, World Population Prospects 2019: Highlights (New York: United Nations, 2019), p. 1.

TREND 5
THE END OF FAMINE

Adequate nutrition is a basic requirement for human survival. Yet for most of history, food was always scarce. The prevalence of food shortages can be gleaned from the profusion of commonly used idioms, such as "feast today, famine tomorrow"; from fairy tales, such as Hansel and Gretel; and from scriptural references, such as the biblical Four Horsemen of the Apocalypse, in which Famine accompanies Pestilence, War, and Death. In fact, the greatest famine of all time occurred between 1958 and 1962, when the Chinese communist ruler Mao Zedong used brute force to nationalize his country's farmland, causing up to 45 million deaths in the process.[22]

Since 1961, the global average population weighted food supply per person per day rose from 2,196 calories to 2,962 calories in 2017.[23] To put these figures in perspective, the U.S. Department of Agriculture recommends that moderately active adult men consume between 2,200 and 2,800 calories a day and moderately active women consume between 1,800 and 2,000 calories a day. In Sub-Saharan Africa, the average food supply per person per day rose from approximately 1,800 calories in 1961 to 2,449 calories in 2017.[24] Put differently, the world's poorest region enjoys access to food that is roughly equivalent to that of the Portuguese in the early 1960s.

What accounts for the growing access to food? First, agricultural productivity has greatly improved because of more scientific methods of farming, access to plentiful and much improved fertilizers and pesticides, and new high-yield and disease-resistant plants. Second,

> "Agricultural productivity has greatly improved because of more scientific methods of farming, access to plentiful and much-improved fertilizers and pesticides, and new high-yield and disease-resistant plants."

the world has grown much richer, and people can afford to buy more food, thus stimulating its production. Third, the spread of democracy and the free press ensures that governments are more accountable and human rights abuses widely reported. Fourth, improved transport and communications allow countries with bountiful harvests to sell or donate their agricultural surpluses to countries suffering from food shortages.

In his 1968 book *The Population Bomb*, Paul Ehrlich, from Stanford University, wrote: "The battle to feed all of humanity is over. In the 1970s hundreds of millions of people will starve to death in spite of any crash programs embarked upon now."[25] That year, the food supply in 34 out of 152 countries surveyed amounted to fewer than 2,000 calories per person per day. That was true of only 2 out of 173 countries surveyed in 2017. Today, famines have all but disappeared outside of war zones.

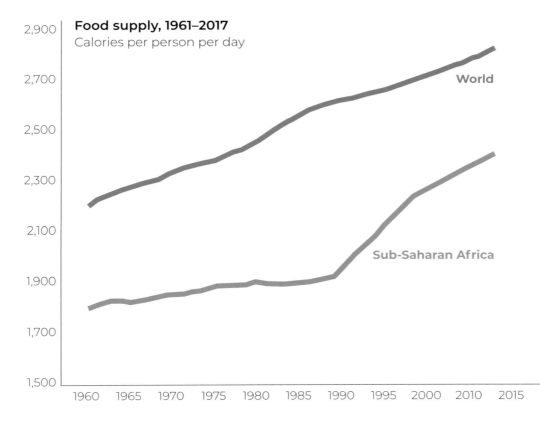

Food supply, 1961–2017
Calories per person per day

World

Sub-Saharan Africa

Source: FAOSTAT, Food Balance Sheets website, UN Food and Agriculture Organization, January 27, 2020.

MORE LAND FOR NATURE

The global tree canopy increased by 2.24 million square kilometers (865,000 square miles) between 1982 and 2016, reported researchers at the University of Maryland in a September 2018 study in *Nature*.[26] That's a land area larger than Alaska and Montana combined.

Using satellite data to track the changes in various land covers, they found that gains in forest area in the temperate, subtropical, and boreal climatic zones are offsetting declines in the tropics. In addition, forest area is expanding even as areas of bare ground and short vegetation are shrinking. Furthermore, forests in mountainous regions are expanding as climate warming enables trees to grow higher up on mountains. A 2011 study in the journal *Nature Climate Change* estimates that global forest growth and regrowth currently act as a carbon sink, annually taking from the atmosphere one-third and

one-fourth of the total carbon dioxide emissions from burning fossil fuels.[27] The tree canopy in Europe, including European Russia, has increased by 35 percent—the greatest gain among all continents. The researchers attribute much of that increase to the "natural afforestation on abandoned agricultural land," which has been "a common process in Eastern Europe after the collapse of the Soviet Union." The tree canopy in the United States and China has increased by 34 percent and 15 percent, respectively.

> "Expanding woodlands suggests that humanity has begun the process of withdrawing from the natural world, which, in turn, will provide greater scope for other species to rebound and thrive."

The study notes that the expansion of the agricultural frontier is the primary driver of deforestation in the tropics where forest cover continues to shrink in countries like Argentina, Brazil, and Paraguay.

These new data are counter to the Food and Agriculture Organization's 2015 findings that forest cover had dropped from 31.6 percent of global land area in 1990 to 30.6 percent in 2015.[28] The disparity between the Maryland and FAO reports arises from the FAO's reliance on data supplied by governments and somewhat different definitions of what counts as forest cover.

Expanding woodlands suggests that humanity has begun the process of withdrawing from the natural world, which, in turn, will provide greater scope for other species to rebound and thrive.

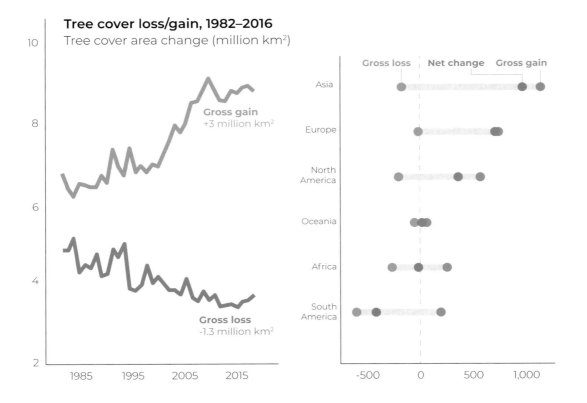

Tree cover loss/gain, 1982–2016
Tree cover area change (million km²)

Gross gain
+3 million km²

Gross loss
-1.3 million km²

Gross loss | Net change | Gross gain

Asia
Europe
North America
Oceania
Africa
South America

-500 | 0 | 500 | 1,000

Source: Xiao-Peng Song et al., "Global Land Change from 1982 to 2016," *Nature* 560, no. 1 (2018): 639.
Note: km² = square kilometers

PLANET CITY

Growing urbanization is good for both humanity and the natural world. Historically, between 80 percent and 90 percent of humanity lived in rural areas and worked in agriculture. As late as 1900, 41 percent of Americans worked on farms. Today, fewer than 2 percent do.[29] Before mechanization, farm work was physically exhausting and poorly paid, which helps to explain why people started to move from the countryside to the cities.

> **"Cities are the centers of innovation, engines of growth, and home to the richest segment of the population— just think of Delhi, London, New York, Shanghai, Seoul, and Tokyo."**

For many people, cities were the engines of liberation. In medieval Europe, for example, serfs who escaped their masters and lived in a city for "a year and a day" became free from servitude. Hence the German saying, *Stadtluft macht frei* (city air makes you free).

Cities are the centers of innovation, engines of growth, and home to the richest segment of the population— just think of Delhi, London, New York, Shanghai, Seoul, and Tokyo. In fact, the World Bank found: "No country has grown to middle income without industrializing and urbanizing. None has grown to high income without vibrant cities."[30] Urbanization is also good for the environment. On average, city dwellers use less electricity, emit less carbon dioxide, and have smaller land footprints than people living in the countryside.

According to the United Nations, the share of humanity living in cities rose from 751 million (29 percent) in 1950 to 4.2 billion (55 percent) in 2018.[31] That still leaves over 3 billion people living in rural areas. The Organisation for Economic Co-operation and Development estimates that 85 percent of the world's population will be urbanized by 2100. That means that fewer than 1.5 billion of a projected global population of 9.8 billion will be living in rural areas by the end of this century.[32]

At least some of the land spared from human habitation will then revert to nature.

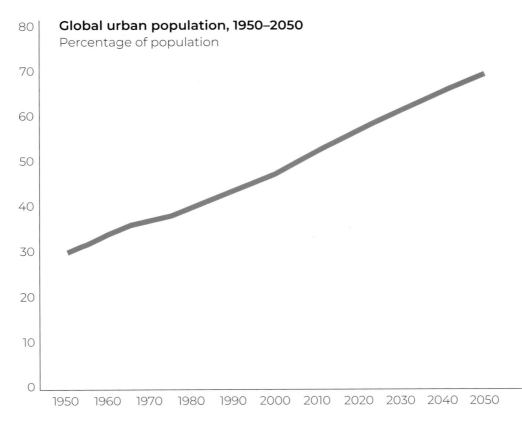

Global urban population, 1950–2050

Percentage of population

Source: United Nations, Department of Economic and Social Affairs, Population Division, *World Urbanization Prospects: The 2018 Revision, Online Edition*, "File 2: Percentage of Population at Mid-Year Residing in Urban Areas by Region, Subregion, Country and Area, 1950–2050," 2018.

DEMOCRACY ON THE MARCH

Reflecting on the implosion of communist dictatorships at the end of the 20th century, American academic Francis Fukuyama suggests in his 1989 essay, "The End of History," "What we may be witnessing is not just the end of the Cold War," but "the universalization of Western liberal democracy as the final form of human government."[33] Today, many accuse Fukuyama of naiveté, because authoritarian populism of left-wing and right-wing varieties is on the rise in many parts of the world; Russia, Turkey, and Venezuela are each

> **"Democracy may not be expanding as fast as it once did, but neither is it in full retreat."**

examples of countries moving away from liberal democracy. Yet it would be a mistake to dismiss Fukuyama's thesis altogether. Democracy may not be expanding as fast as it once did, but neither is it in full retreat.

Modern representative democracy arose in Western Europe during the 18th century. It then slowly spread to other parts of the world, reaching a high point in the early 1920s. The rise of fascism and communism reversed some of the democratic gains in the decades afterward. By the early 1970s, roughly twice as many countries could have been described as autocratic than as democratic. After the fall of the Berlin Wall in 1989, democracy greatly expanded.

The Center for Systemic Peace evaluates the characteristics of a political regime in each country on a scale from −10, which denotes a tyranny like North Korea, to 10, which denotes a politically free society like Norway. The percentage of countries that scored 7 and above, thus qualifying as full-fledged democracies, rose from 31 percent in 1989 to 49 percent in 2017. The percentage of countries that scored −7 and below, thus qualifying as full-fledged autocracies, declined from 39 percent to 11 percent over the same period. Countries with both democratic and autocratic characteristics rose from 30 percent to 39 percent.[34] All in all, it is premature to write democracy's obituary just yet.

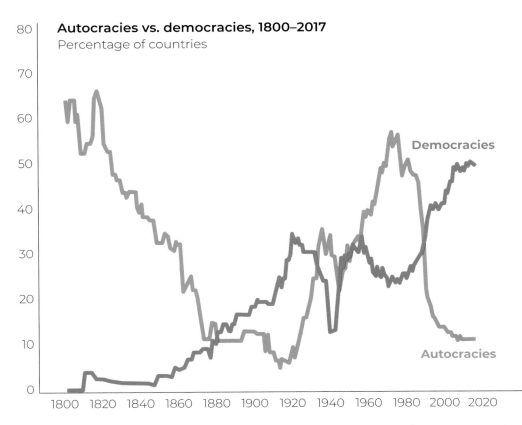

Autocracies vs. democracies, 1800–2017
Percentage of countries

Democracies

Autocracies

Source: Monty G. Marshall and Gabrielle Elzinga-Marshall, "Global Report 2017: Conflict, Governance, and State Fragility," Center for Systemic Peace, Vienna, VA, August 27, 2017.

THE LONG PEACE

Over the past half century, wars between countries have become rarer, and those that do occur kill fewer people. A 2017 RAND Corporation report on global trends in warfare observes: "The incidence of armed conflict in the world ha[s] actually *decreased* substantially in the past few decades, although spiking up in 2014–2015. Interstate war (that is, war between states) has become a rare event."[35]

One common way to measure the global trend in armed conflicts is to count annually the pairs of countries that are engaged in warfare with one another. The decades after World War II saw a wave of decolonization along with the collapse of the Soviet Empire in the 1990s, resulting in the number of sovereign countries growing from approximately 50 in 1946 to nearly 200 today. Intuitively it would seem that the possibility of war between sovereign countries might rise as their numbers multiplied. However, the trend in the number of interstate wars has generally been downward since the end of World War II. A Clingendael Institute report points out that the trend in interstate warfare has declined as more countries have become simultaneously democratic, wealthy, and economically intertwined in recent years.[36] As a result, our relatively pacific era has been characterized as the "democratic" or the "capitalist" peace. The 2017 RAND Corporation report also projects through 2040 that interstate wars will likely continue to decline.

> "Over the past half century, wars between countries have become rarer, and those that do occur kill fewer people."

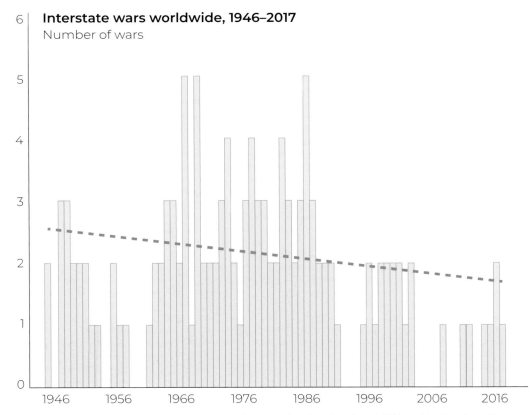

Interstate wars worldwide, 1946–2017
Number of wars

Sources: Stephan De Spiegeleire, Khrystyna Holynska, and Yevhen Sapolovych, "Things May Not Be as They Seem: Geo-Dynamic Trends in the International System," in Strategic Monitor 2018–2019, eds. Tim Sweijs and Danny Pronk (The Hague: Clingendael Institute, 2019), Figure 10.

A SAFER WORLD

The chance of a person dying in a natural catastrophe—earthquake, flood, drought, storm, wildfire, landslide, or epidemic—has declined by nearly 99 percent since the 1920s and 1930s.[37] People today are much more likely to survive natural disasters because of increased wealth and technological progress. Buildings are better constructed to survive earthquakes; weather satellites and sophisticated computer models provide early storm warnings that give people time to prepare and evacuate; and broad disease surveillance enables swift medical interventions to halt developing epidemics.

Unfortunately, bad weather and earthquakes produce death and destruction largely when they encounter poverty. Consequently, 90 percent of deaths from natural disasters occurred in developing and poor countries between 1996 and 2015.[38] The largest natural disasters in the past 20 years were the Indian Ocean tsunami that resulted in the deaths of 230,000 people in 2004, the 2010 Haitian earthquake in which 223,000 people died, and Cyclone Nargis, a Category 4 storm that killed 138,000 people in Myanmar in 2008. In contrast, when Queensland, Australia, was hit by the Category 5 Cyclone Yasi in 2010, the result was zero fatalities.[39]

> "People today are much more likely to survive natural disasters because of increased wealth and technological progress."

The costs of weather-related catastrophes like hurricanes have increased, largely because rising incomes have prompted people to put more property in harm's way as they build more houses, roads, schools, factories, and shopping centers. Nevertheless, University of Colorado political scientist Roger Pielke Jr. has found that the global trend in weather-related disaster losses between 1990 and 2017 as a proportion of global gross domestic product is downward.[40] Globally speaking, people are generally getting richer faster than nature can destroy their property.

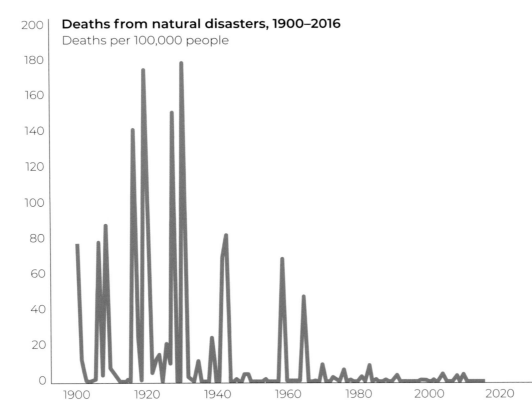

Deaths from natural disasters, 1900–2016
Deaths per 100,000 people

Sources: Centre for Research on the Epidemiology of Disasters, Emergency Events Database website, 2019; and Centre for Research on the Epidemiology of Disasters and United Nations Office for Disaster Risk Reduction, "Poverty and Death: Disaster Mortality, 1996–2015," 2016, p. 112.

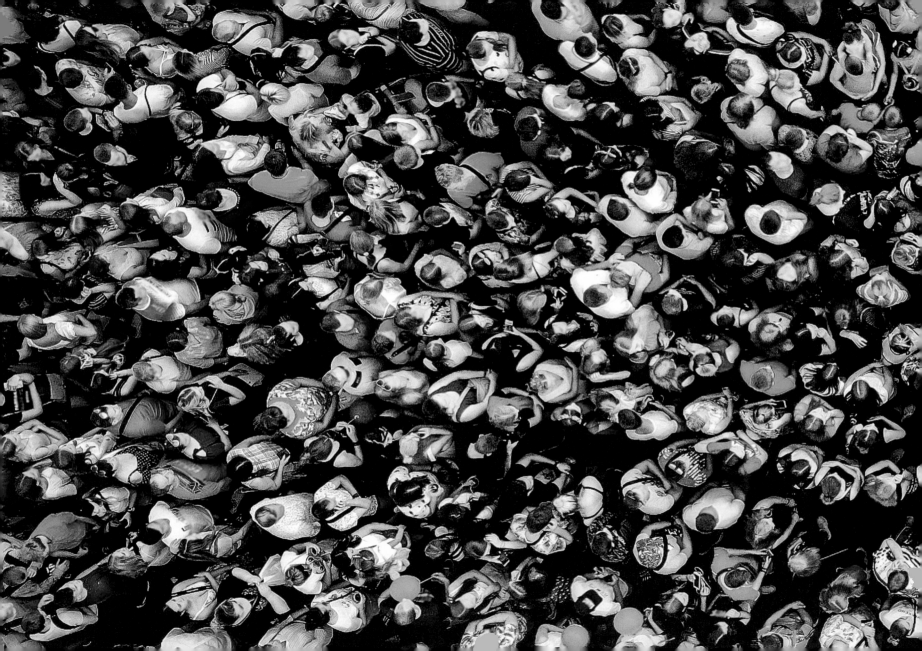

PEOPLE TRENDS

LIFE OPTIONS ARE EXPANDING

The Human Development Index (HDI) was created in 1990 by researchers at the United Nations Development Programme to emphasize that the expansion of human choices should be the ultimate criterion for assessing development results. The HDI is formulated on a scale of 0 to 1 by taking into account each country's life expectancy at birth; its mean years of schooling for adults and the expected years of schooling for its children; and its national income per capita in purchasing power parity dollars. Purchasing power parity is defined as the ratio of prices in national currencies of the same good or service in different countries.

The latest Human Development Report notes that the HDI for the world as a whole increased from 0.598 in 1990 to 0.728 in 2017. That is to be expected given the improving global trends in life expectancy, education, and income documented in other chapters of this book. The report also calculates that between 1990 and 2017, the HDI for developing countries rose from 0.515 to 0.681. That's an astonishing 32 percent improvement in just 27 years. The HDI average for the highly developed member countries of the Organisation for Economic Co-operation and Development (OECD) increased from 0.785 to 0.895. Since HDI in developing countries is growing more than twice as fast as

> **"Since HDI in developing countries is growing more than twice as fast as that in OECD countries, the HDI gap between the two is shrinking fast."**

that in OECD countries, the HDI gap between the two is shrinking fast.[41]

In 2017, Norway achieved the highest HDI score ever measured, at 0.953, because its average life expectancy was 82.3 years and per capita income was $68,012 per year. Its mean and expected years of schooling stood at 12.6 and 17.9, respectively. The overall lowest HDI was scored by Niger at a dismal 0.354, because life expectancy in that country was 60.4 years, and average per capita income was $906 per year. Its mean and expected levels of schooling were, respectively, 2 and 5.4 years.

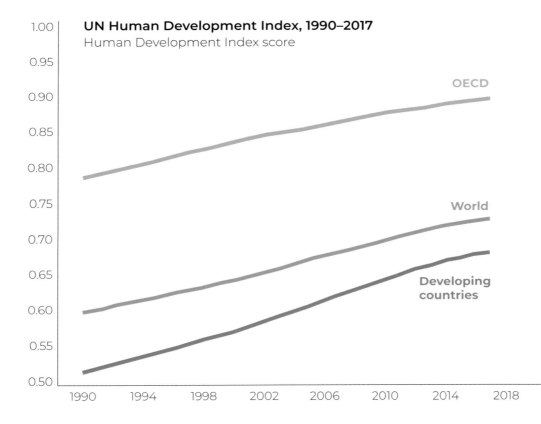

UN Human Development Index, 1990–2017
Human Development Index score

OECD

World

Developing
countries

1.00
0.95
0.90
0.85
0.80
0.75
0.70
0.65
0.60
0.55
0.50

1990   1994   1998   2002   2006   2010   2014   2018

Source: UN Development Programme, Human Development Reports, 2018, Table 2.
Note: OECD = Organisation for Economic Co-operation and Development.

GLOBAL HAPPINESS IS RISING

People around the world are generally becoming happier with their lives. In six waves of polls since 1981, the World Values Survey (WVS) has asked respondents, "Taking all things together, would you say you are very happy, quite happy, not very happy, or not at all happy?"[42]

University of Michigan sociologist Ronald Inglehart, founder of the WVS, reports in his 2018 book *Cultural Evolution* that ascending levels of subjective well-being correlate strongly

> "Ascending levels of subjective well-being correlate strongly with rising per capita income, rising levels of democracy, and increasing social liberalization as expressed by growing tolerance for racial, sexual, and religious outgroups."

with rising per capita income, rising levels of democracy, and increasing social liberalization as expressed by growing tolerance for racial, sexual, and religious outgroups.[43] Those three factors combine to broaden the range of free choices available to people, thus enhancing happiness.

Using WVS data from all 12 countries that have been regularly surveyed from 1981 through 2014—Argentina, Australia, Finland, Germany, Japan, Mexico, the Netherlands, South Africa, South Korea, Spain, Sweden, and the United States— Inglehart reports that average global happiness has been rising. This result is in line with the data reported in this book showing that the world has been experiencing remarkable increases in income, democratization, and social tolerance over the past four decades.

Citing happiness survey data for 14 wealthy countries from the 1950s,

economist Richard Easterlin argued in 1974 that almost no correlation existed between rising national per capita income and rising happiness. Inglehart points out that subsequent research has overturned this apparent paradox and finds that the residents of wealthier nations are indeed happier than those of poorer nations. In addition, richer people in a given country are happier than their less well off fellow citizens. And finally, as countries get richer, their people do indeed become happier. More money may not buy happiness, but the two do correlate.[44]

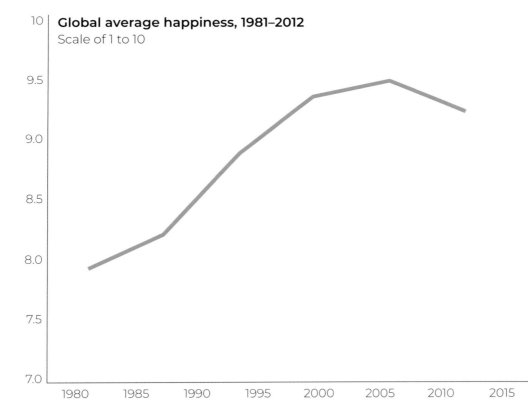

Global average happiness, 1981–2012
Scale of 1 to 10

Source: Ronald F. Inglehart, *Cultural Evolution: People's Motivations Are Changing, and Reshaping the World* (Cambridge: Cambridge University Press, 2018), p. 156.

TREND 13

GLOBAL INCOME IS RISING

Economic historian Angus Maddison, at the University of Groningen, spent his adult life estimating gross domestic product (GDP) figures for the world over the past two millennia. According to Maddison's calculations, the average global income per person per year stood at $800 in year 1 of the Common Era (2011 U.S. dollars). That's where it remained for the next thousand years. This income stagnation does not mean that economic growth never happened. Growth did occur, but it was low, localized, and episodic. In the end, economic gains always petered out.

In 1800, average global income stood at roughly $1,140 per person per year. Put differently, over the course of the 18 centuries that separated the birth of Christ and the election of Thomas Jefferson to the U.S. presidency, income rose by about 40 percent.

The advent of the Industrial Revolution in the late 18th century changed everything. Between 1800 and 1900, GDP per person per year rose from $1,140 to $2,180. In other words, humanity made over twice as much progress in 100 years as it did in the previous 1,800 years.

In 2008, the last year in Maddison's final estimates, average global income per person per year stood at $13,172. That means that the real standard of living rose by more than tenfold between 1800 and 2008.

Maddison died in 2010, but a group of his colleagues continues his work. The latest edition of the GDP estimates came out in 2018. Although Maddison's original numbers changed slightly, the long-term trend in income growth remained almost identical. The Maddison Project's 2018 estimates show that in 1900, GDP per person per year amounted to $2,021 (as opposed to Maddison's $2,180). By 2016, income had risen to $14,574 per person per year. That amounts to a 621 percent increase since 1900.

Finally, the Maddison Project's 2018 estimates show that average global income per person per year rose at a compound annual rate of 1.72 percent between 1900 and 2016. If that trend continues, average global income will reach an inflation-adjusted $60,955 per person per year in 2100 (all figures are in 2011 U.S. dollars).

> "The advent of the Industrial Revolution in the late 18th century changed everything . . . humanity made over twice as much progress in 100 years as it did in the previous 1,800 years."

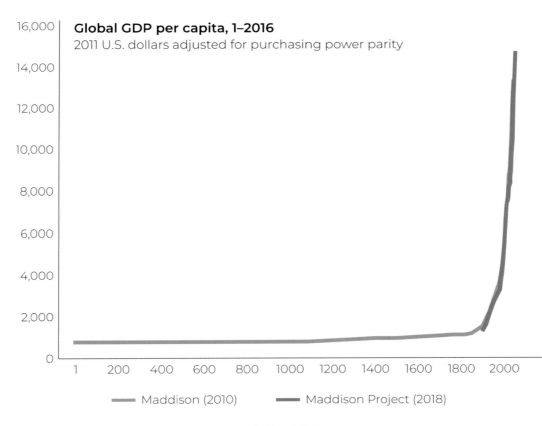

Global GDP per capita, 1–2016
2011 U.S. dollars adjusted for purchasing power parity

Maddison (2010)   Maddison Project (2018)

Source: Angus Maddison Project Database 2010 and 2018

GLOBAL INCOME INEQUALITY IS FALLING

Inequality is the handmaiden of progress, explains Princeton University economist Angus Deaton in his book *The Great Escape: Health, Wealth, and the Origins of Inequality*. Only when some people become better-off does a higher standard of living for the many become imaginable. That is precisely what happened during the Industrial Revolution, when a pronounced income gap started to emerge between the countries of Western Europe and North America on the one hand and the rest of the world on the other hand. In recent decades, however, global inequality has started to decline—primarily due to faster growth in non-Western countries.

"Global inequality has started to decline—primarily due to faster growth in non-Western countries."

The most commonly used indicator of income inequality is the Gini coefficient, which measures income inequality on a scale of 0 (i.e., all incomes are equal) to 1 (i.e., one person has all the income). One way to measure global income inequality, explains Branko Milanovic from City University of New York, is to calculate a population weighted average of Gini values for all individual countries. Data show that global income inequality started to decline in the 1980s, coterminous with a period of greater economic freedom and interconnectedness known as "globalization."

That measure of income inequality—let's call it "inequality between countries"—is somewhat misleading, however, for it ignores the fact that some income inequality is also found within any given country. As a result, some of the inequality across the world will not be counted by this measure. To get a sense of "inequality across the human race," income inequality between countries has to be adjusted by income "inequality within countries." On that measure, global income inequality begins to decline somewhat later—after the beginning of the new millennium.

Still, both measures of global income inequality show a downward trend. As such, concludes Milanovic, we are seeing "the first decline in inequality between world citizens since the Industrial Revolution."[45]

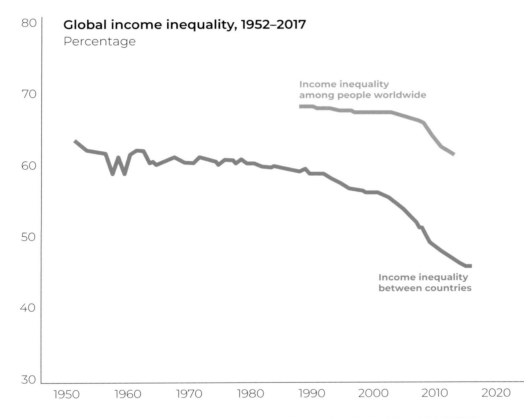

Global income inequality, 1952–2017
Percentage

Income inequality
among people worldwide

Income inequality
between countries

Source: Branko Milanovic, personal communication with the author (Marian L. Tupy), July 12, 2019.

THE EVOLUTION OF SLUMS

As a general rule, slum dwellings lack access to improved water and sanitation, sufficient living area, security of tenure, durability, and adequate protection of their inhabitants from the elements. In 1990, 47 percent of the world's urban population lived in slums. That figure fell to 30 percent by 2014. South Asia made the greatest progress in reducing its slum population, from 57 percent to 31 percent; East Asia and the Pacific saw a decline from 47 percent to 26 percent; Latin America and the Caribbean from 36 percent to 20 percent; and Sub-Saharan Africa from 67 percent to 55 percent.[46]

The total number of people living in slums, however, continues to increase because of the extremely rapid speed of urbanization throughout the developing world. According to the United Nations' *World Cities Report 2016*, the number of slum dwellers increased from 689 million in 1990 to 881 million in 2014. Some of the greatest concentrations of slum dwellers include Orangi Town, Karachi, Pakistan (2.4 million); Ciudad Neza, Mexico City, Mexico (1.2 million); Dharavi, Mumbai, India (1 million); Kibera, Nairobi, Kenya (700,000); and Khayelitsha, Cape Town, South Africa (400,000).[47]

In the short to medium term, provision of clean water and improved sanitation to slum dwellers ought to be a priority for governments and the private sector in developing countries. In the long run, if the ultimately successful process of urbanization in the West is any guide, rising incomes will enable people in poor countries to move from slums into proper dwellings on their own.

> "In 1990, 47 percent of the world's urban population lived in slums. That figure fell to 30 percent by 2014."

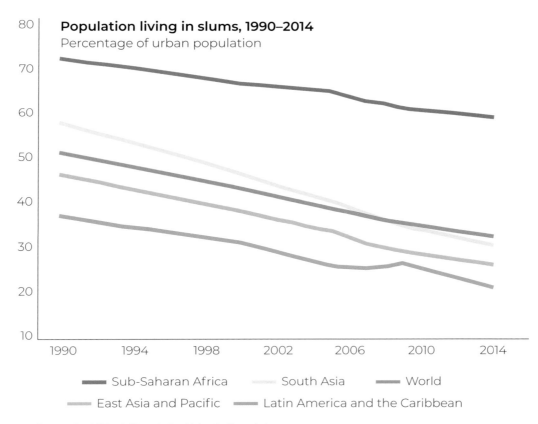

Population living in slums, 1990–2014
Percentage of urban population

- Sub-Saharan Africa
- South Asia
- World
- East Asia and Pacific
- Latin America and the Caribbean

Source: World Bank, "Population Living in Slums" chart.

EMPOWERING WOMEN

Women account for half of the world's population, yet they have held political power only infrequently. Notwithstanding great female rulers of the past, including Elizabeth I, Catherine the Great, Hatshepsut, Victoria, and Cleopatra, politics used to be dominated by men to a much greater degree than is the case today. That began to change with the enfranchisement of women, beginning at the end of the 19th century. The

> **"The political empowerment of women came about as a consequence of the Enlightenment, which emphasized equality for all, as well as the growing economic power and independence of women that resulted from the Industrial Revolution."**

political empowerment of women came about as a consequence of the Enlightenment, which emphasized equality for all, as well as the growing economic power and independence of women that resulted from the Industrial Revolution.

Of the extant countries, New Zealand was the first to acknowledge women's right to vote in 1893. Australia did the same in 1901. The first European country to introduce women's suffrage was Finland in 1906. Norway followed in 1913, and Denmark in 1915. By the end of World War I, women in Canada, Russia, Germany, and Poland also had a vote. British women won the right to vote in 1918, and American women in 1920. Switzerland was the last European country to legalize women's suffrage, in 1971. Today, women vote in all countries except the Vatican City State,

where only cardinals have the right to elect the pope, and of course in some countries, elections remain substantially meaningless.[48]

In 1960, Sirimavo Bandaranaike of Sri Lanka became the world's first democratically elected female prime minister. In 1980, Vigdís Finnbogadóttir of Iceland became the world's first democratically elected female president. Between 1960 and 2018, 73 countries have had at least one female leader.[49] In 1990, 12.7 percent of seats in national parliaments were held by women. That number rose to 23.7 percent in 2017. The highest share of female representatives in national parliaments was in Latin America and the Caribbean (29.3 percent), and the lowest was in the Middle East and North Africa (16.2 percent).[50]

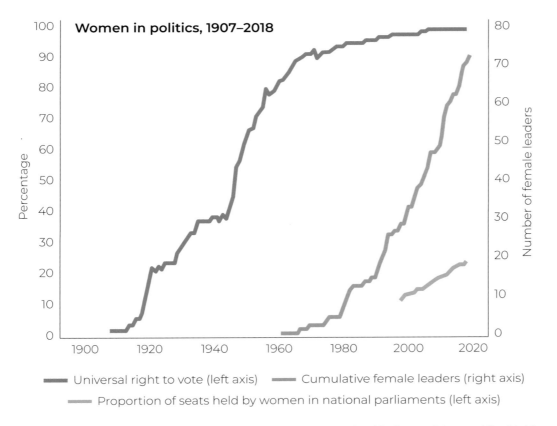

Women in politics, 1907–2018

Percentage (left axis)
Number of female leaders (right axis)

— Universal right to vote (left axis) — Cumulative female leaders (right axis)
— Proportion of seats held by women in national parliaments (left axis)

Sources: World Bank, "Proportion of Seats Held by Women in National Parliaments" chart; and Our World in Data, "Share of Countries Having Achieved Different Milestones in Women's Political Representation" chart, 2017.

CHOOSING SMALLER FAMILIES

The world population grew from 1.6 billion in 1900 to 7.7 billion in 2019, not because people are breeding like rabbits but because they are no longer dropping like flies.

Most women gave birth to an average of six to eight children throughout most of human history.[51] Despite those high fertility rates, the world population increased very slowly because of high death rates. Until the 19th century, nearly 60 percent of children died from disease, starvation, or violence before reaching adulthood.

The death rate for children begins dropping in the 19th century in some Western countries where medicine, sanitation, and nutrition improved, and economic growth accelerated.

"The global fertility rate will continue falling as more women can anticipate living longer and more interesting lives."

Although their mortality rates were falling, their fertility rates for a time remained high. The result was a period of rapid population increase. By the mid-20th century, most developed countries had experienced the "demographic transition" from high birth and death rates to low birth and death rates.

By the second decade of the 21st century, most countries have already passed through their demographic transitions or are well on the way to doing so.

University of Connecticut anthropologists Nicola Bulled and Richard Sosis report that when women can expect to live to between 40 and 50 years of age, they bear an average of 5.5 children. When their life expectancy rises to between 61 and 71 years, total fertility drops to 2.5 children; and over an average lifespan of 75 years, women average 1.7 children.[52] Longer female life expectancy is a powerful indication of improved economic and social conditions. Thus, more women choose to have fewer children because they reasonably expect most of their children will survive to adulthood.

Education and productive work outside the home also reduce fertility. Schooling opens more options for women, while market employment increases women's opportunity cost of taking care of children. Female life expectancy exceeds 75 years in all but 2 (Bhutan and North Korea) of the 87 countries with below-replacement fertility. Demographers generally define replacement fertility as an average of 2.1 children born per woman. At this rate, a population can replace itself from one generation to the next without migration from other countries.

Global fertility rates plummeted from 5 in 1960 to 2.43 children today as global average life expectancy for women increased from 53 to 72 years. The global fertility rate will continue falling as more women can anticipate living longer and more interesting lives.

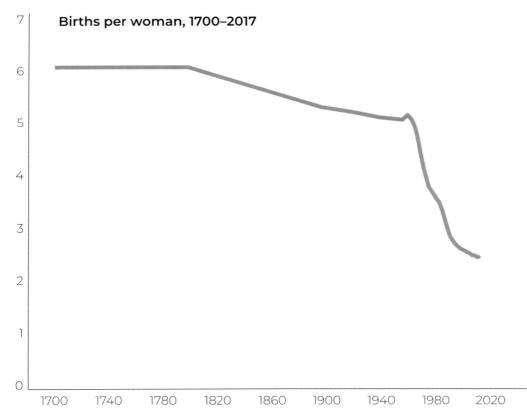

Births per woman, 1700–2017

Sources: For data prior to 1961, see Ronald Lee, "The Demographic Transition: Three Centuries of Fundamental Change," *Journal of Economic Perspectives* 17, no. 4 (2003): 168, table 1; and for 1961–2017 data, see World Bank World Development Indicators, "Fertility Rate, Total (Births per Woman)," chart.

ACHIEVING UNIVERSAL LITERACY

Nearly 90 percent of the world's population in 1820 was illiterate. Today almost 90 percent can read. The United Nations Educational, Scientific, and Cultural Organization (UNESCO) broadly defines literacy as "the ability to identify, understand, interpret, create, communicate and compute using printed and written materials."[53] A common benchmark of literacy, to give just one example, is the ability to read a newspaper. Being able to read and write is associated with reduced poverty rates, decreased mortality rates, greater gender equality, lower fertility rates,

> "Being able to read and write is associated with reduced poverty rates, decreased mortality rates, greater gender equality, lower fertility rates, and increased political awareness and participation."

and increased political awareness and participation. According to the UNESCO *Global Education Monitoring Report*, if all students in low-income countries left school with elementary reading skills, 171 million people could be lifted out of poverty.[54]

Global progress toward universal literacy over the past two centuries has been uneven. By 1940, more than 90 percent of the people living in the United States, Canada, Australia, Western Europe, and Eastern Europe were literate. In contrast, only about 42 percent of the populations of Latin America and East Asia could read. At that time, the rates of literacy in the Middle East and North Africa, South and Southeast Asia, and Sub-Saharan Africa were about 15 percent, 11 percent, and 10 percent, respectively. Given these regional disparities, the global literacy rate in 1940 was still below 50 percent.

According to the World Bank, the global literacy rate among men ages 15 and older was about 77 percent in 1970, rising to nearly 90 percent by 2016. Among women, that number rose from 61 percent to 83 percent over the same period. In 2016, nearly 90 percent of women between the ages of 15 and 24 were literate. That number was almost 93 percent among men of the same age.[55] Clearly, literacy gaps between rich and poor countries, and men and women, are closing.

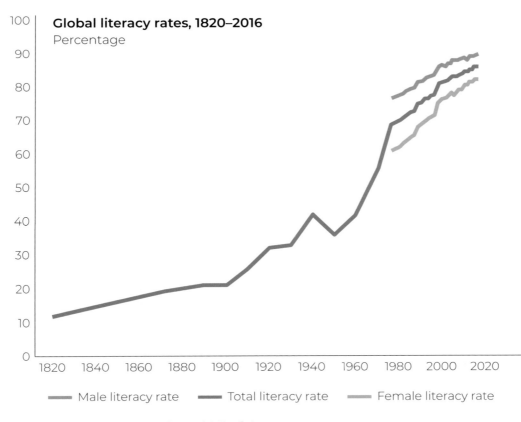

Global literacy rates, 1820–2016
Percentage

Male literacy rate　　Total literacy rate　　Female literacy rate

Source: World Bank, "Literacy Rate, Adult Total" chart.

MORE KIDS IN SCHOOL

Rising incomes across the globe have liberated increasing numbers of children from the obligation to work in fields and factories, which was formerly necessary to support their families. Consequently, school enrollment has been rising worldwide.

The gross school enrollment rate is the ratio of the number of students who live in a country to those who qualify for each particular grade level. Because some students in primary

> **"A 2014 World Bank study calculated that another year of schooling raises an individual's earnings by about 9 percent a year."**

and secondary school will be overage, underage, or grade repeaters, the gross rate can exceed 100 percent. The gross tertiary enrollment rate takes into account the number of young people in the five-year age group following the leaving age for secondary school, which is usually 18. That means that the tertiary figure is commonly well below 100 percent.

According to World Bank figures, the gross primary enrollment rate has increased from 89 percent in 1970 to 104 percent in 2017.[56] A greater percentage of students around the world are also now attending high school. The gross secondary enrollment rate rose from 41 percent in 1970 to

77 percent in 2017.[57] College enrollments are up significantly too. In 1970, the gross enrollment rate was just 10 percent. In 2017, the global rate had increased to 37 percent.[58]

A 2014 World Bank study calculated that another year of schooling raises an individual's earnings by about 9 percent a year.[59] Schooling thus enhances the virtuous circle in which higher incomes enable parents to afford even more educational opportunities for their children.

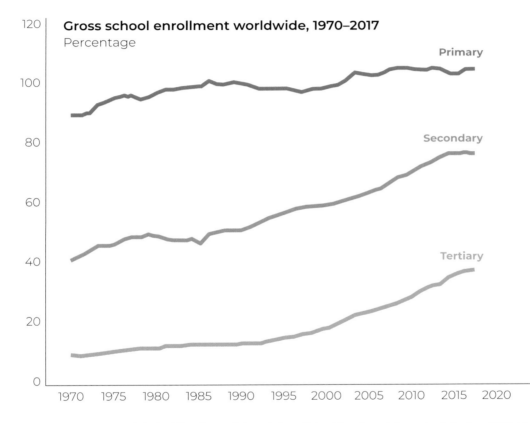

Gross school enrollment worldwide, 1970–2017
Percentage

Primary

Secondary

Tertiary

120

100

80

60

40

20

0

1970 1975 1980 1985 1990 1995 2000 2005 2010 2015 2020

Sources: World Bank, "School Enrollment, Primary" chart; "School Enrollment, Secondary" chart; and "School Enrollment, Tertiary" chart.

MORE YEARS IN SCHOOL

Throughout most of history, education was by and large limited to a small sliver of urban-dwelling, freeborn men, and included clergy, imperial administrators, tax collectors, and merchants. Peasants—who constituted between 80 percent and 90 percent of the population in much of the world until the Industrial Revolution—were too poor to pay for schooling. In any case, low agricultural productivity meant that everyone, including the peasants' children, had to work the land to produce enough food to survive.

As late as 1870, the total length of schooling at all levels of education for people between the ages of 25 and 64 is estimated to have been only about 0.5 years.[60] In a handful of outliers, such as Switzerland and the United States, it was as high as four years. In France and the United Kingdom, it averaged less than one year. In the world's less developed regions, such as Africa and Asia, schooling remained negligible.

By 2010, Robert Barro from Harvard University and Jong-Wha Lee from Korea University estimated that the global average length of schooling at all levels of education stood at 8.56 years.[61] That year, primary, secondary, and tertiary schooling amounted to 4.85 years, 3.23 years, and 0.48 years, respectively. By 2040, the four measures of schooling will increase to 10.52 years (total), 5.03 years (primary), 4.69 years (secondary), and 0.8 years (tertiary).

A new study in the *Lancet* estimates that in 2040 the global life expectancy will reach 74 years for men and 80 years for women.[62] That means that men will spend over 14 percent of their lives in school, whereas women will spend over 13 percent of their lives in school. Contrast those statistics with 2010. That year, global life expectancy for men and women was 68.6 years and 72.8 years, respectively. That means that men and women spent 12.5 percent and 11.8 percent, respectively, of their lives learning.

Economists, including Barro himself, note a robust correlation between education and economic growth. The lengthening of schooling, in other words, is one of the reasons for humanity's great enrichment over the past 200 years or so.

> **"The lengthening of schooling . . . is one of the reasons for humanity's great enrichment over the past 200 years or so."**

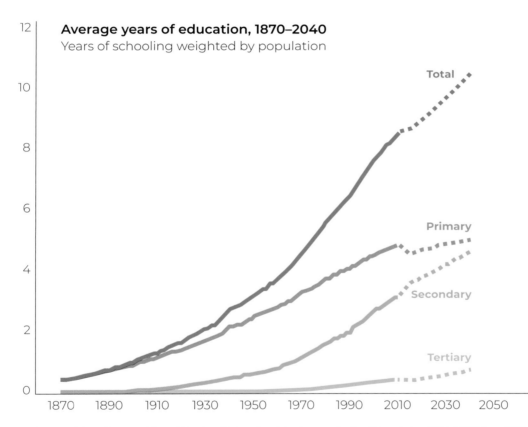

Average years of education, 1870–2040
Years of schooling weighted by population

Total

Primary

Secondary

Tertiary

Source: Robert Barro and Jong-Wha Lee, "Educational Attainment for Total Population, 1950–2010," June 2018 update.

IQ SCORES RISING MASSIVELY

In the course of the past century, people all over the world have been getting a lot smarter. In that time, the average IQ score of each generation has increased, so IQ tests are "renormed" (made harder) every 15–20 years by resetting the mean score to 100. In the 1980s, New Zealand political scientist James Flynn realized that the renorming all went in one direction: upward at a rate of about 3 points per decade.[63] This insight meant that a person with an average score of 100 in 1965 would likely score just 85 points on current tests. Since then, Flynn's discovery of generally rising IQs has been validated in scores of studies encompassing both rich and poor countries around the globe. In 2015, an article in the journal *Perspectives on Psychological Science* measured worldwide IQ gains between 1909 and 2013, based on 271 independent samples totaling almost 4 million participants from 31 countries.[64] The study confirmed that average IQ test scores have increased by 30 points over the past century.

What accounts for this massive increase in IQ scores? Researchers suggest a panoply of causes, including better nutrition, exposure to more mentally challenging media, more formal schooling, and, thanks to better sanitation and higher vaccination rates, the reduced load of infectious childhood diseases. Mobilizing the immune system to fight off diseases and parasites is very expensive metabolically, taking away nutrients and energy that would otherwise be used to fuel the building and maintenance of a growing child's brain.

Some more recent studies have detected a topping out and even a slight reversal of the Flynn effect in some richer countries.[65] However, a 2018 study reports that the United States continued to show a steady average IQ gain from 1989 to 2014 at about its historic rate of 0.3 IQ points per year.[66]

> "Average IQ test scores have increased by 30 points over the past century."

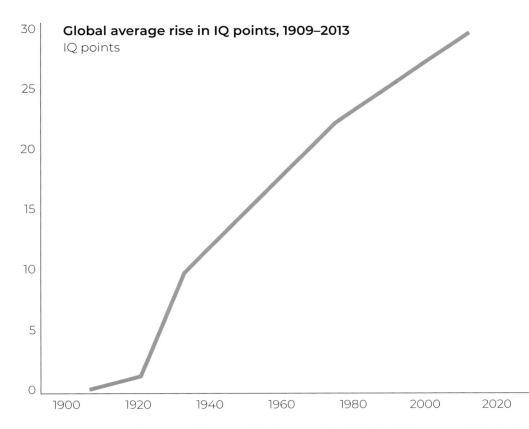

Global average rise in IQ points, 1909–2013
IQ points

Source: Jakob Pietschnig and Martin Voracek, "One Century of Global IQ Gains: A Formal Meta-Analysis of the Flynn Effect (1909–2013)," *Perspectives on Psychological Science* 10, no. 3 (2015): 285.

DECRIMINALIZING LGBTQ

Homosexuality has existed in all human societies and is also common in the animal kingdom. Yet with a few exceptions—such as ancient Athens, where same-sex attraction between men was tolerated in a highly restricted form—homosexuality has generally been frowned on, discouraged, and punished. As such, countless gay men and women suffered deep psychological anguish, imprisonment, torture, and death on account of their sexual orientation. In 1791, the Kingdom of France became the first nation to decriminalize homosexual behavior. That measure was an outcome of the Enlightenment, an intellectual movement that popularized the notion that private activities among consenting adults were none of anyone else's business. A few more countries followed suit, but it was not until the sexual revolution of the 1960s that decriminalization of homosexuality gained steam.

Toleration of homosexuality today tends to be highly correlated with the level of urbanization, education, and income. People in urban and intellectually vibrant settings tend to be more frequently exposed to and accepting of unorthodox lifestyles. Similarly, relatively wealthy people—who are no longer concerned with existential challenges, such as avoidance of violence and access to adequate nutrition—tend to be more concerned with questions of "fairness," which include equal rights for gays and lesbians.

Out of the 193 members of the United Nations in 2019, consensual same-sex sexual acts were legal in 123 countries, illegal in 68 countries, and de facto illegal in 2 countries.[67] Although some regions, such as the Middle East and Africa, lag behind the rest of the world when it comes to the treatment of homosexuals, increasing urbanization, education, and wealth are likely to make people everywhere more socially tolerant in the future.

> **"Out of the 193 members of the United Nations in 2019, consensual same-sex sexual acts were legal in 123 countries, illegal in 68 countries, and de facto illegal in 2 countries."**

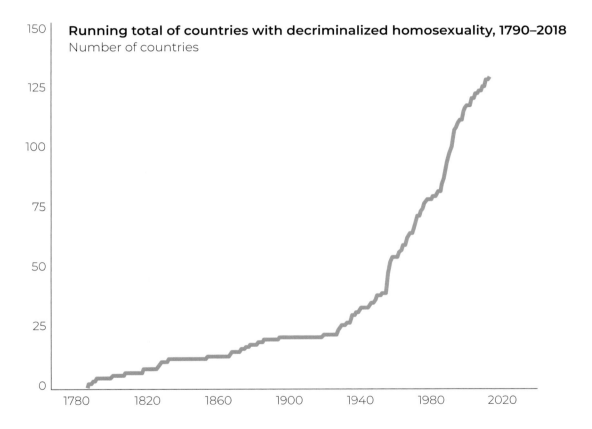

Running total of countries with decriminalized homosexuality, 1790–2018
Number of countries

150

125

100

75

50

25

0

1780   1820   1860   1900   1940   1980   2020

Source: Lucas Ramón Mendos, *State-Sponsored Homophobia*, 13th ed. (Geneva: International Lesbian, Gay, Bisexual, Trans and Intersex Association, 2019), dataset.

GLOBAL FREE PRESS PROGRESS, WITH SETBACKS

No human right is more important than free speech. Without it, no other rights can be asserted and defended. Free speech—the right of anyone to criticize and evaluate the claims of anyone else—is the best environment for discovering political, social, economic, and scientific truths. Political, religious, and ideological absolutists and authoritarians cannot tolerate criticism that punctures and wounds their delusions and dogmas. They look for ways to silence the offensive speakers, including imprisonment and murder.

Freedom House, an independent think tank based in Washington, DC, has been publishing its annual *Freedom of the Press* report on media independence around the world since 1980. During that time, it has documented a significant global upswing in press freedom. In 1986, Freedom House reported that in only 24 percent of countries were the media free from government control, and 55 percent had no free press. The rest had a partially free press. By 2006, Freedom House reported that the share of countries with a free press had increased to 38 percent, whereas the not-free fraction had fallen to 32 percent.[68] In its latest 2017 report, the think tank's researchers unhappily note that the global trend toward greater press freedom has recently been set back somewhat. By 2016, only 31 percent of countries enjoyed a free press. In 33 percent, the media were not free. The rest were partly free.[69]

What is the future of press freedom? In a free society, people can pursue and propound their own versions of the truth. In a despotic, fear-based society, everyone must submit to and live with lies. Societies in which citizens can speak freely flourish; societies where speech is muzzled by despots shrivel.

> **"Societies in which citizens can speak freely flourish; societies where speech is muzzled by despots shrivel."**

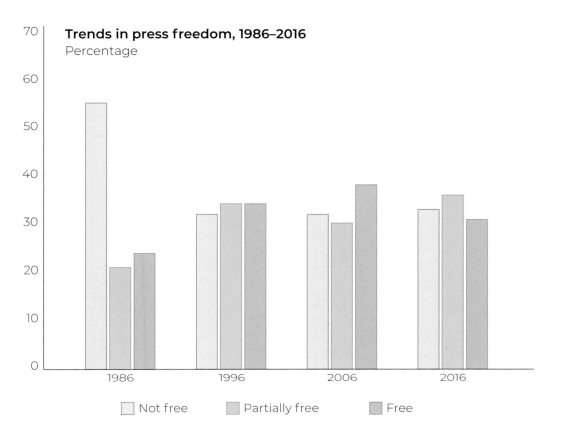

Trends in press freedom, 1986–2016
Percentage

Legend: Not free · Partially free · Free

Source: Freedom House, "Freedom of the Press 2017: Press Freedom's Dark Horizon," 2017.

LIFE EXPECTANCY IS RISING

Average life expectancy at birth for people hovered at about 30 years for most of human history. The reason was mostly that about one-third of children died before they reached their fifth birthday. Demographers estimate that in 16th-century England, 60 out of 100 children would die before the age of 16. Some fortunate people did have long lives, but only 4 percent of the world's population generally lived to be older than 65 years before the 20th century.

In 1820, global average life expectancy was still about 30 years. Remarkably, around that time, life expectancy in Europe and North America began rising at the sustained rate of about three months per year. That increase was largely a consequence of better nutrition and deployment of public health measures, such as filtered water and sewers.

During the past 200 years, global life expectancy has more than doubled, now reaching more than 72 years according to the World Bank.[70] Worldwide, the proportion of people who are 65 years old and older has also more than doubled, to 8.5 percent. For the first time in human history, people ages 65 and older will by 2020 outnumber children under age 5.

> "During the past 200 years, global life expectancy has more than doubled, now reaching more than 72 years according to the World Bank."

Even in the rapidly industrializing United States, average life expectancy was still only 47 years in 1900, and only 4 percent of people were 65 years old and older. U.S. life expectancy is now 78.7 years.[71] And today 15.6 percent of Americans are older than 65, whereas only 6.1 percent are younger than 5.[72]

Life expectancy's rising by three months annually implies a global average lifespan of 92 years by 2100. However, the 2017 United Nations medium fertility scenario more conservatively projects that average life expectancy will rise from 72 years today to 83 years by the end of this century.[73]

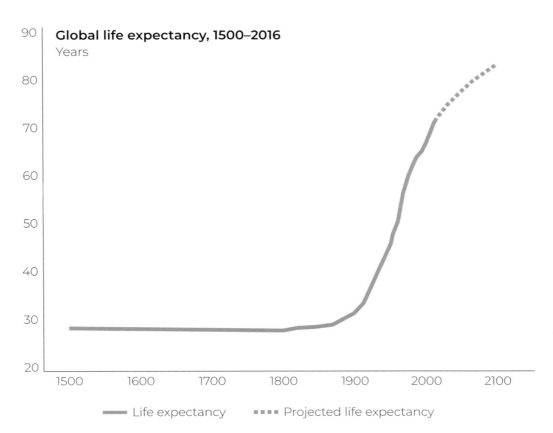

Global life expectancy, 1500–2016
Years

Life expectancy ━━━ Projected life expectancy ▪▪▪▪

Sources: For 1500–1950 data, see Angus Maddison, *The World Economy, Volume 1* (Paris: OECD Development Centre, 2006), 33, table 1-5b; and for 1951–2016 data, see World Bank, *World Development Indicators*, "Life Expectancy at Birth, Total (Years)" chart.

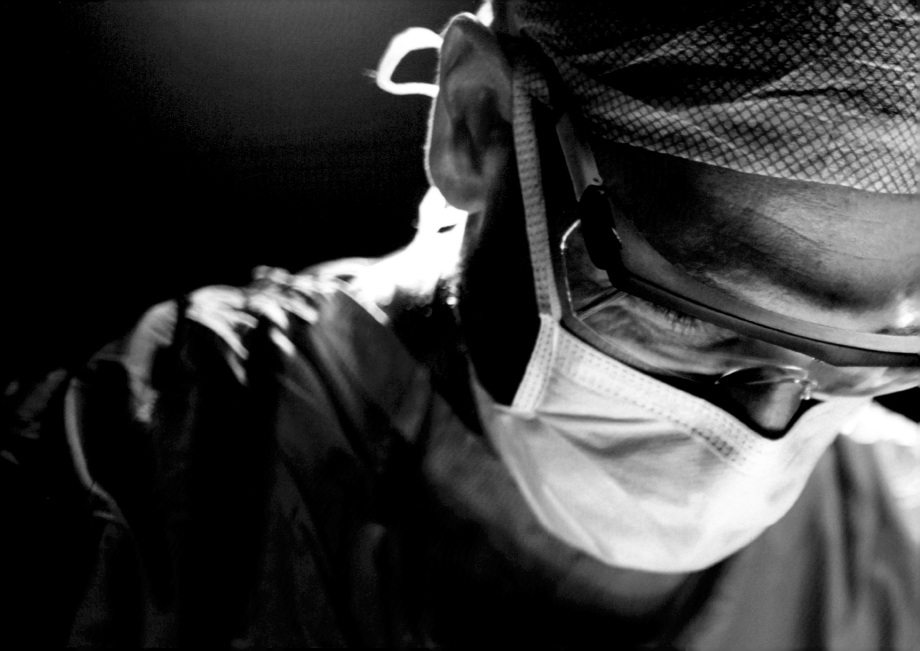

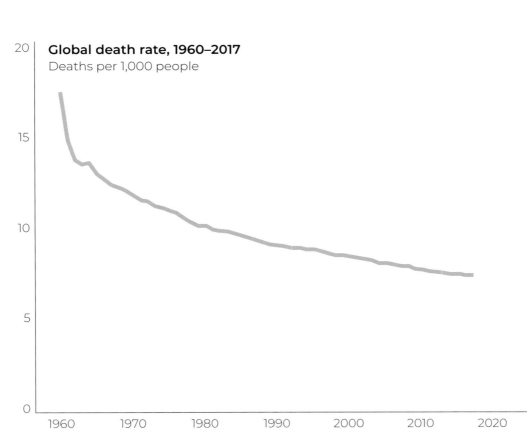

Global death rate, 1960–2017
Deaths per 1,000 people

20

15

10

5

0

1960   1970   1980   1990   2000   2010   2020

Source: World Bank, "Death Rate, Crude" chart.

VASTLY FEWER CHILDREN DIE YOUNG

Demographers estimate that in premodern societies, out of every 1,000 babies born, about 300 died before reaching their first birthday.[77] Most of those infants succumbed to infectious diseases and malnutrition. By 1900, infant mortality rates had fallen to approximately 140 per 1,000 live births in modernizing countries, such as the United Kingdom and the United States. Infant mortality rates in the two countries continued to fall to about 56 per 1,000 live births in 1935 and down to about 30 per 1,000 live births by 1950. In 2017, the UK and U.S. infant mortality rates were, respectively, 3.8 and 5.9 per 1,000 live births. Since 1900, in other words, infant mortality in those two countries has fallen by more than 95 percent.

In the past few decades, infant mortality rates have been falling steeply in the rest of the world. The World Health Organization estimates that the global infant mortality rate was just under 160 per 1,000 live births in 1950. By 1990, the agency reports that the global infant mortality rate had dropped to 64.8 per 1,000 live births. In 2017, the global infant mortality rate was down to 29.4 per 1,000 live births, about the level of the United Kingdom and the United States in 1950.

> "Access to modern medicine, including childhood vaccinations, is a major factor in falling infant mortality rates."

Vastly fewer babies are dying today, because rising incomes have enabled more people to take advantage of improved sanitation and nutrition and more countries to devote more resources toward better educating mothers. Access to modern medicine, including childhood vaccinations, is a major factor in falling infant mortality rates. In 2015, the United Nations adopted a set of Sustainable Development Goals, including reduction of the global infant mortality rate to 12 per 1,000 live births by 2030.[78]

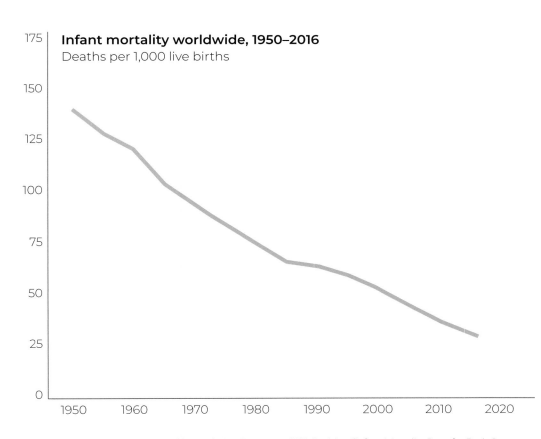

Infant mortality worldwide, 1950–2016
Deaths per 1,000 live births

Source: United Nations, *World Population Prospects, 2019 Revision*, "Infant Mortality Rate, for Both Sexes Combined (Infant Deaths per 1,000 Live Births)" table.

TREND 27

MOTHERS ARE LIVING LONGER

The World Health Organization defines maternal mortality as "the death of a woman while pregnant or within 42 days of termination of pregnancy."[79] Such deaths can occur for a variety of reasons, including bleeding and infection after childbirth, high blood pressure during pregnancy, complications during delivery, and unsafe abortions. Early statistics are difficult to come by, but British parish records indicate a maternal mortality rate of 1,000 per 100,000 live births in the first half of the 18th century. Since women were pregnant more often than is the case today, the actual risk of dying from pregnancy complications would have been much higher.

In the mid-19th century, Hungarian physician Ignaz Semmelweis noticed that women who gave birth at home died at a lower rate than women who were assisted by doctors. He hypothesized that doctors, who did not wash their hands, passed diseases from other patients to pregnant women. Unfortunately, Semmelweis's insight was strenuously opposed until, several years later, French biologist Louis Pasteur established a definitive link between germs and disease in the 1860s.

After doctors started to disinfect their hands, maternal mortality began to fall, first in Western countries and later in the rest of the world. The global maternal death rate fell from 385 per 100,000 live births in 1990 to 216 in 2015. That's a reduction of 44 percent. In Sub-Saharan Africa, the world's poorest region, the number of maternal deaths fell from 987 to 547 over the same period—a reduction of 45 percent.

Similar declines took place in all other geographical regions, and the United Nations expects that the maternal mortality rate will fall to 70 per 100,000 live births by 2030.[80] A somewhat disappointing and hopefully temporary exception is North America, where the U.S. maternal death rate rose from a minuscule 12 per 100,000 live births to 14. The increase in the U.S. maternal mortality rate seems to be driven by the rise in opioid addiction, which complicates pregnancy, as well as women becoming pregnant much later in life and resorting to more risky C-section child deliveries.

> "After doctors started to disinfect their hands, maternal mortality began to fall, first in Western countries and later in the rest of the world."

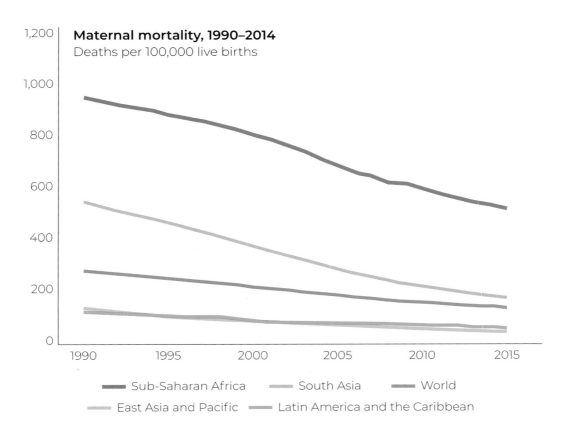

Maternal mortality, 1990–2014
Deaths per 100,000 live births

Legend:
- Sub-Saharan Africa
- South Asia
- World
- East Asia and Pacific
- Latin America and the Caribbean

Source: World Bank, *World Development Indicators*, "Maternal Mortality Ratio (National Estimate, per 100,000 Live Births)" chart.

TREND 28
VACCINES ARE SAVING LIVES

Before its eradication in 1979, smallpox was one of humanity's oldest and most devastating scourges. The disease—which can be traced all the way back to pharaonic Egypt—was highly contagious. A 1775 French medical textbook, for example, estimated that 95 percent of the population contracted smallpox at some point during their lives. In the 20th century alone, the disease is thought to have killed between 300 million and 500 million people. The smallpox mortality rate among adults was between 20 percent and 60 percent. Among infants, it was 80 percent. Those figures partly explain why life expectancy remained between 25 and 30 years for so long.

Edward Jenner, an English country doctor, noted that milkmaids never got smallpox. He hypothesized that milkmaids' exposure to cowpox protected them from the much more deadly disease. In 1796, Jenner inserted cowpox pus from the hand of a milkmaid into the arm of a young boy. Jenner later exposed the boy to smallpox, but he remained healthy. *Vacca* is the Latin word for cow—hence the root of the English word "vaccination." An organized effort by national governments, international organizations, nongovernmental organizations, and the private sector during the second half of the 20th century has brought a plethora of vaccines to the world's most distant communities, thereby alleviating a

"The World Health Organization estimates that vaccines prevented at least 10 million deaths between 2010 and 2015 alone. Many millions more lives were protected from illness."

great amount of human suffering. The World Health Organization estimates that vaccines prevented at least 10 million deaths between 2010 and 2015 alone. Many millions more lives were protected from illness. As of 2018, global vaccination coverage remains at 85 percent, with no significant changes during the past few years. That said, an additional 1.5 million deaths could be avoided if global immunization coverage improves.[81]

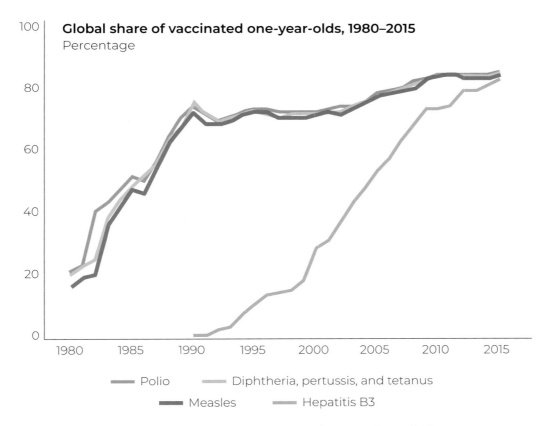

Global share of vaccinated one-year-olds, 1980–2015
Percentage

Legend:
- Polio
- Diphtheria, pertussis, and tetanus
- Measles
- Hepatitis B3

Source: Our World in Data, "Global Vaccine Coverage: Share of Vaccinated 1-Year-Olds."

OVERCOMING HIV/AIDS

AIDS (acquired immunodeficiency syndrome) is a range of progressively worsening medical conditions caused by infection with HIV (human immunodeficiency virus) that, if left untreated, culminates in death. In the main, HIV spreads through unprotected sex, contaminated blood transfusions, and hypodermic needles, as well as from mother to child during pregnancy, delivery, and breastfeeding. Scientists believe that HIV is an offshoot of SIV (simian immunodeficiency virus)—a virus that attacks the immune system of monkeys and apes. It is thought that the virus "jumped" from simians to humans in the 1920s when Congolese hunters came in contact with animal blood.[82]

The first countries to document cases of people infected with HIV include Congo in 1959, Norway in 1966, and the United States in 1969. In its early days, the disease spread primarily within the gay community, with infection rates of 5 percent among homosexual men in New York and San Francisco

in 1978. The disease was first covered by the mainstream press in 1981 and named one year later. Over time, the disease has come to affect everyone, with heterosexual men and women accounting for the vast majority of the 76 million people who have been infected with the virus and the 35 million people who have died from AIDS over the past 40 years.

The first drugs slowing the progression of HIV appeared in the mid-1990s. Today, the disease can be treated with highly active antiretroviral therapy, which not only slows the disease's progression, but also decreases the risk of HIV transmission from one person to another.

The HIV pandemic peaked in the mid-2000s, when some 1.9 million people died of AIDS each year. In 2017, fewer than 1 million died from the sickness. In the mid-1990s, some 3.4 million new HIV infections occurred each year. In 2017, only 1.8 million new HIV infections were documented. In 2017, 37 million

people were living with HIV. That year, 59 percent of those living with the disease had access to treatment.[83]

In 2000, the highly active antiretroviral therapy cost more than US$10,000 per patient per year. "Within a year," the United Nations found, the price "plummeted to US$350 per year when generic manufacturers began to offer treatment. Since then, owing to competition among quality-assured generic manufacturers, the cost of treatment continued to fall."[84] In 2016, it stood at US$64 per patient per year Even the world's poorest people, such as those in Sub-Saharan Africa, enjoy access to drugs courtesy of Western aid, especially the U.S. President's Emergency Plan for AIDS Relief.

"The HIV pandemic peaked in the mid-2000s, when some 1.9 million people died of AIDS each year. In 2017, fewer than 1 million died from the sickness."

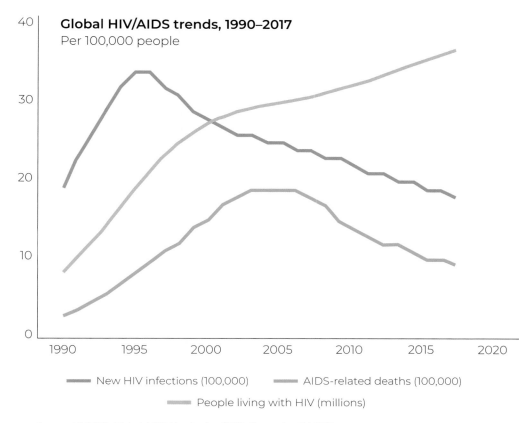

Global HIV/AIDS trends, 1990–2017
Per 100,000 people

— New HIV infections (100,000)   — AIDS-related deaths (100,000)
— People living with HIV (millions)

Source: UNAIDS, Global AIDS Monitoring 2020, December 24, 2019.

TROUNCING TUBERCULOSIS

Tuberculosis is an infectious disease caused by the bacterium *Mycobacterium tuberculosis*. The disease spreads through coughing, spitting, and sneezing, and it usually affects the lungs of the victim. Most infections are latent and present no symptoms. However, in roughly 10 percent of cases, the disease progresses into an active phase that, if left untreated, has a 50 percent mortality rate.

Tuberculosis was responsible for the illnesses and deaths of many famous people, including Tutankhamun, Cardinal Richelieu, Molière, Spinoza, Goethe, Friedrich Schiller, Sir Walter Scott, Paganini, Simón Bolívar, Keats, Emerson, Edgar Allan Poe, Chopin, Thoreau, all three Brontë sisters, Dostoyevsky, Gauguin, Chekhov, Kafka, Eleanor Roosevelt, D. H. Lawrence, George Orwell, and Nelson Mandela.

In 2017, the World Health Organization reported, 10 million people fell ill with tuberculosis and 1.6 million died from the disease. Eight countries—Bangladesh, China, India, Indonesia, Nigeria, Pakistan, the Philippines, and South Africa—accounted for two-thirds of all new tuberculosis cases.[85] Tuberculosis prevention and control efforts include vaccination of children and detection and treatment of active cases of the disease.

Globally, the incidence of tuberculosis declined from 173 per 100,000 population in 2000 to 140 in 2016. That's a 19 percent reduction. In Sub-Saharan Africa, it declined from

"Tuberculosis prevention and control efforts include vaccination of children and detection and treatment of active cases of the disease."

333 to 255 cases, or 23 percent. South Asia—the other region most affected by tuberculosis—saw a decline from 274 to 215, or 22 percent.[86] Meanwhile, the global detection rate of tuberculosis rose from 35 percent in 2000 to 65 percent in 2016.[87] That means that even as detection improved substantially, the known incidence still declined. Finally, the global tuberculosis treatment success rate rose from 69 percent in 2000 to 83 percent in 2015.[88]

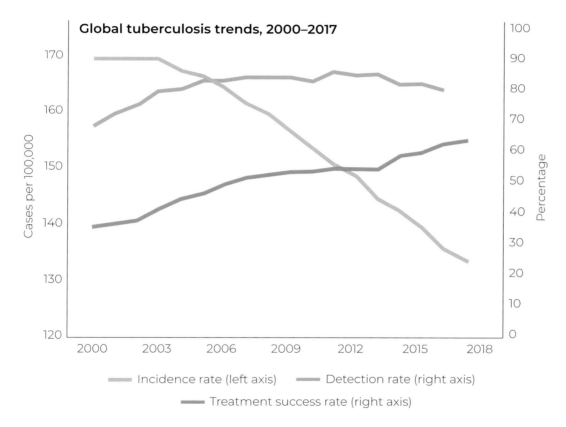

Global tuberculosis trends, 2000–2017

Incidence rate (left axis) — Detection rate (right axis)

Treatment success rate (right axis)

Sources: World Bank, *World Development Indicators*, "Incidence of Tuberculosis (per 100,000 People)" chart; "Tuberculosis Case Detection Rate (%, All Forms)" chart; and "Tuberculosis Treatment Success Rate (% of New Cases)" chart.

MALARIA RETREATS

Malaria kills hundreds of thousands of people each year—many of them children. In addition to death and human suffering, malaria retards economic development in poor countries by reducing overall labor productivity, discouraging investments and tourism, and impairing schooling because of high degrees of absenteeism among students and teachers. Researchers estimate that the economic costs of malaria range from 0.41 percent of gross domestic product in Ghana to a staggering 8.9 percent in Chad.[89] Moreover, it is estimated that in the absence of malaria and HIV, foreign direct investment in the median Sub-Saharan African country could rise by as much as a third, thus generating higher growth and more economic opportunities for the local population.

The word "malaria" comes from the Italian words for bad (*mal*) and air (*aria*), for it was thought that the disease was caused by foul air emanating from swamps and bogs. In 1897, Ronald Ross, a British physician, identified mosquitoes as carriers of the disease. Early efforts to control the spread of malaria included draining swamps where mosquito larvae hatched and installing window screens on human dwellings. The invention of the world's first long-lasting synthetic insecticide DDT (dichlorodiphenyltrichloroethane) in the mid-20th century greatly accelerated the fight against the disease. Spraying small amounts of the insecticide on the inside walls of houses repelled, irritated, or killed the mosquitoes. In the 1960s, the use of DDT was restricted when researchers discovered that it had unintended deleterious effects on some wildlife, especially some bird species.

Subsequently, new medicines and insecticides, and the use of insecticide-treated bed nets, became more popular. Mosquitoes are apt to develop resistance to new insecticides relatively quickly, so new tools—such as vaccines and genetically altered mosquitoes—might be needed in the future. Nevertheless, progress in the fight against malaria is being made. According to the Institute for Health Metrics and Evaluation, deaths from malaria declined from 673,000 in 1990 to 620,000 in 2017.[90] In the meantime, the world's population rose from 5.39 billion to 7.53 billion. That means that the malaria death rate dropped from 12.6 per 100,000 in 1990 to 8.2 per 100,000 in 2017.

> "Progress in the fight against malaria is being made. According to the Institute for Health Metrics and Evaluation, deaths from malaria declined from 673,000 in 1990 to 620,000 in 2017."

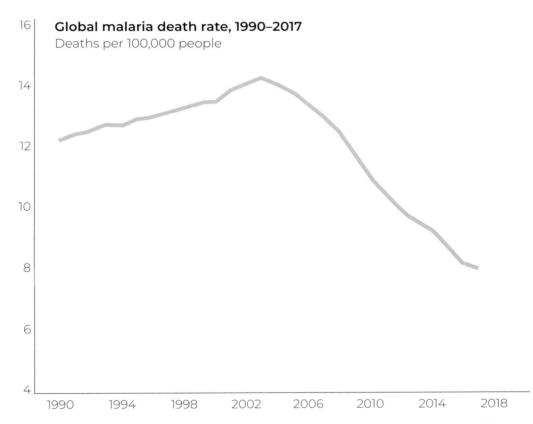

Global malaria death rate, 1990–2017
Deaths per 100,000 people

Source: Institute for Health Metrics and Evaluation, "GBD Results Tool; Location: Global; Year: 1990–2017; Cause;
Age: All Ages; Metric: Number; Measure: Deaths; Sex: Both; Cause: A.4.1 Malaria," Global Burden of Disease
Study results, 2017.

72

WINNING THE WAR ON CANCER

Cancer is a class of some 100 diseases that are characterized by abnormal cell growth. In 2018, cancers killed 9.6 million people, according to the World Health Organization. That number was 68 percent more than in 1990, when 5.7 million people died from cancer. In 2018, lung cancer killed 1.76 million people. Colorectal cancer killed 862,000 people, stomach cancer killed 783,000 people, liver cancer killed 782,000 people, and breast cancer killed 627,000 people. Globally, about one in six deaths was caused by cancer. Roughly 70 percent of all cancer deaths occurred in the developing world, where the quality of medical care lags behind that in the developed world.[91]

The longer people live, the more likely the normally orderly process of cell division is to spin out of control, and cancer will ensue. Put differently, the risk of dying from cancer increases with age. In 2017, for example, 46 percent of people who died from cancer were older than 70 years of age, and 41 percent were between 50 and 69 years old. Writing in 2017, Max Roser from Oxford University noted, "Collectively, children and adolescents under 14 years old account for around one percent of cancer deaths—although still tragically, this equates to around 110,000 children per year."[92] Cancers today are detected more speedily through increasingly sophisticated screening tests, medical imaging, and biopsy. They are treated by constantly improving drug regimens and, increasingly, highly personalized cancer treatments. Roser—who adjusted the total number of cancer deaths by population growth and increased lifespans—found that "despite increasing numbers of cancer deaths, individual death rates are falling. In 1990, 161 people out of every 100,000 globally died from cancer—by 2016 this had fallen to 134 per 100,000." That's a reduction of 17 percent, or roughly 0.7 percent per year.[93]

> "Cancers today are detected more speedily through increasingly sophisticated screening tests, medical imaging, and biopsy. They are treated by constantly improving drug regimens and, increasingly, highly personalized cancer treatments."

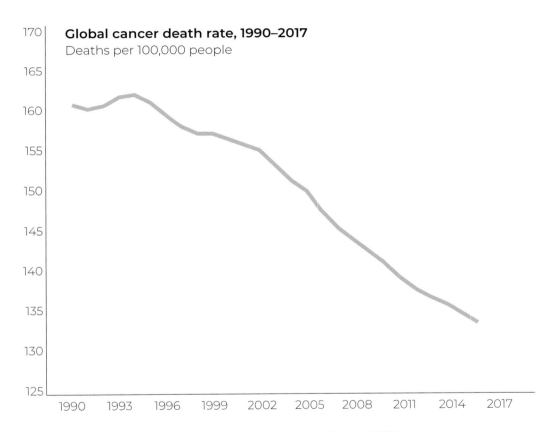

Global cancer death rate, 1990–2017
Deaths per 100,000 people

Source: Max Roser and Hannah Ritchie, "Cancer," Our World in Data, April 2018 update.

TOBACCO'S LAST STAND

Today, we know that smoking tobacco causes 90 percent of lung cancer deaths, but for thousands of years, people smoked with reckless abandon in the Americas. Tobacco smoking originated in Mesoamerica, from which it spread, thanks to the Columbian exchange, to the Old World. By the middle of the 17th century, every major civilization embraced smoking, often in the face of hostile authorities, who tried to stamp out the practice through heavy taxation or outright prohibition.

People use tobacco for many different reasons, including stress relief and social bonding. Nicotine, a stimulant found in tobacco, increases the levels of dopamine and adrenaline, thus leading to feelings of pleasure and excitement. Although highly addictive, nicotine is relatively harmless, which is why people who wish to stop smoking are encouraged to chew nicotine gum and use nicotine patches. It is the burning of

tobacco, and inhalation of tar and toxic gases, that causes cancer.

In 1949, Richard Doll from the British Medical Research Council and Bradford Hill from the London School of Hygiene started to look at lung cancer patients in London hospitals. They found that out of 649 patients with lung cancer, only 2 were nonsmokers. Additional research confirmed significantly higher rates of lung cancer among smokers than nonsmokers. By the early 1960s, the first restrictions on smoking began to appear, including bans on the sale of cigarettes to children and on smoking in public places.

> **"By the early 1960s, the first restrictions on smoking began to appear, including bans on the sale of cigarettes to children and on smoking in public places."**

Because of population growth, the absolute number of daily smokers has continued to grow, rising from 720 million in 1980 to 967 million in 2012. Over the same period, however, the estimated prevalence of daily smokers fell from 25.1 percent to 18.6 percent of the world's population. Between 2000 and 2015, the share of women over the age of 15 who smoked (even occasionally) fell from 11 percent to 6.4 percent. Among men, that number fell from 44 percent to 35 percent over the same period.[94]

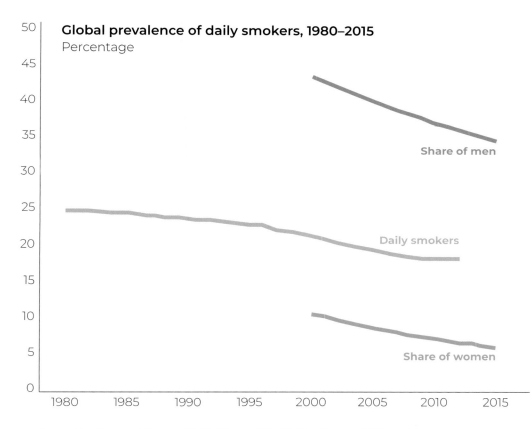

Global prevalence of daily smokers, 1980–2015
Percentage

Share of men

Daily smokers

Share of women

Source: Max Roser and Hannah Ritchie, "Cancer," Our World in Data, April 2018 update.

ACCELERATING VACCINE DISCOVERIES

Humanity has suffered from deadly diseases for millennia without fully knowing what they were, how they were transmitted, or how they could be cured. Smallpox, which killed between 300 million and 500 million people in the 20th century alone, originated in either India or Egypt at least 3,000 years ago. But it was not until the late 18th century that the English physician Edward Jenner vaccinated his first patient against the disease. It took another two centuries before smallpox was finally eradicated in 1980.

In contrast, modern biomedical progress enabled us to respond to the COVID-19 pandemic in months, not centuries. On December 31, 2019, a cluster of "pneumonia" cases was reported in Wuhan, China. By January 12, 2020, Chinese scientists had identified, sequenced, and made the responsible coronavirus' genetic code publicly available.

That enabled the rest of the world to devise diagnostic tests for the disease. For example, after South Korea identified its first COVID-19 infection on January 20, biotech companies rushed to produce test kits. The kits were available at 50 locations around the country by February 7.

By mid-April, thousands of researchers throughout the world were using digital and biomedical technologies to pursue promising paths toward victory over the disease. Some 200 different programs were underway to develop therapies and vaccines to combat the pandemic.

On December 2, 2020, the United Kingdom became the first country to authorize the use of a vaccine developed by the American Pfizer Corporation and the German BioNTech company. The vaccine, which is 95 percent effective, contains messenger RNA (mRNA) that COVID-19 uses to construct the proteins that enable the virus to infect human cells. The injected

> **"Modern biomedical progress enabled us to respond to the COVID-19 pandemic in months, not centuries."**

mRNA tricks the cell into making these spike proteins, which then induce the immune system to produce antibodies against the virus. Antibodies bind themselves onto attacking viruses, disabling them or marking them for death for other parts of the immune system to deal with.

Modern medicine has enabled humanity to eradicate, nearly eradicate, and otherwise limit the spread of various diseases, including cholera, diphtheria, measles, rubella, and typhoid. Unlike previous vaccines, which tended to use a weaker form of a virus to protect the recipients, the Pfizer/BioNTech vaccine uses the human body itself to achieve the same result. This new technology possibly marks the beginning of a new era of speedy development of highly effective vaccines that will protect humanity in the decades to come. Less than 12 months separated the discovery of COVID-19 and the production of an effective life-saving vaccine. This modern miracle is a testament to human ingenuity.

Speed of vaccine development, 1500 BCE–2020

Polio: 3,348 years

Smallpox: 3,296 years

Cholera: 2,345 years

Typhoid: 2,326 years

Measles: 1,471 years

Rubella: 352 years

Diphtheria: 281 years

Ebola: 43 years

COVID-19: 1 year

1500 BCE   1   2020

Year

Sources: Wikipedia's entries on "Malaria," "Polio," "Cholera," "Typhoid fever," "Measles," "Rubella," "Diptheria,"
"Ebola," and "Coronavirus Disease 2019."

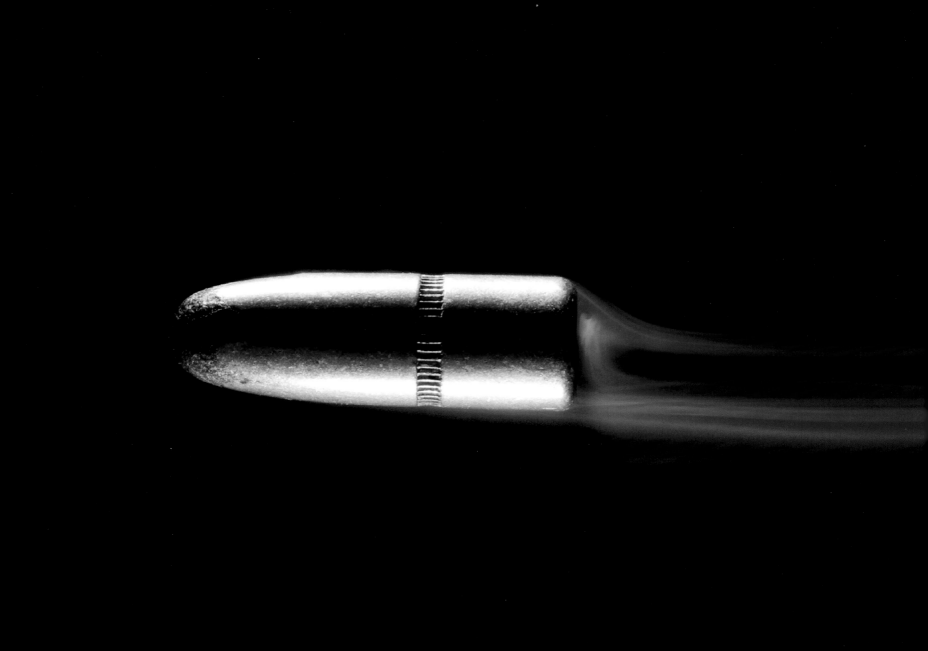

VIOLENCE TRENDS

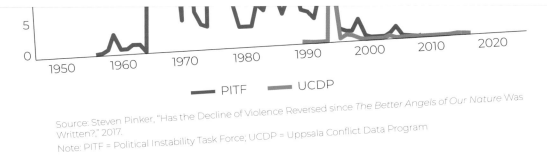

Source: Steven Pinker, "Has the Decline of Violence Reversed since *The Better Angels of Our Nature* Was Written?," 2017.
Note: PITF = Political Instability Task Force; UCDP = Uppsala Conflict Data Program

GENOCIDES ARE DISAPPEARING

According to Frank Chalk and Kurt Jonassohn from Concordia University, ~~~ killings of unarmed civilians

Genocides, notes Harvard University psychologist Steven Pinker in his 2018 book *Enlightenment Now: The Case ~~~ Science, Humanism, and*

49 people per 100,000. The Cambodian Killing Fields of 1975–1979 are likewise visible on the graph to the right, constituting a mass killing of 2 million ~~~ ~~~ Rwandan

TREND 39

MILITARY SPENDING RATIO FALLING

In 1960, global spending on the military was 6 percent of world gross domestic product (GDP). By 2017, it had fallen to 2.2 percent. That's a reduction of 63 percent. Traditionally, the Middle East and North Africa had the highest military spending as a share of GDP, which peaked at 12.3 percent in 1991. In 2017, it stood at 5.7 percent. That's a 54 percent decline. Next came North America, which spent 8.4 percent of its GDP on the military in 1962. In 2017, it spent 3 percent—a decline of 64 percent. Military spending in Europe and Central Asia declined from

> **"If military spending kept pace with economic growth, the world's military expenditures in 2017 would amount to a staggering $3.2 trillion."**

4.5 percent in 1960 to 1.7 percent in 2017—a reduction of 62 percent.[105]

Military spending in South Asia peaked at 4 percent in 1987. Last year, it stood at 2.5 percent. Sub-Saharan Africa spent the most on the military in 1975 (4 percent). In 2017, that figure stood at a paltry 1.3 percent. Finally, military spending in East Asia and the Pacific peaked at 1.9 percent in 1982. Last year, it stood at 1.7 percent of GDP.

Note that in actual dollars, military spending continues to rise. The Stockholm International Peace Research Institute, for example, estimates that between 1988 and 2017, global military spending rose from $1.424 trillion to $1.686 trillion (figures are in 2016 U.S. dollars).[106] That amounts to an appreciation of 18 percent. Over the same period, however, the world's

economy grew from $35.5 trillion to $80 trillion (figures are in 2010 U.S. dollars). That's an increase of 125 percent. If military spending kept pace with economic growth, the world's military expenditures in 2017 would amount to a staggering $3.2 trillion.

VIOLENCE TRENDS

GLOBAL MURDER RATE IS FALLING

Lethal violence was pervasive throughout the world until relatively recently. The best evidence for national murder rates comes from Europe, where extensive records were kept going back centuries. Cambridge University criminologist Manuel Eisner cites data in his 2003 article "Long-Term Historical Trends in Violent Crime," suggesting that the annual homicide rate in 15th-century England hovered at about 24 per 100,000; Dutch homicide rates during the same time are estimated at between 30 and 60 per 100,000; and Swedish homicide rates ranged from 10 to 60 cases per 100,000 between the mid-15th and the mid-17th centuries. Interpersonal violence was ubiquitous in premodern Italy. Fourteenth-century Florence experienced the highest known annual homicide rate of 150 per 100,000, and estimated homicide rates in 16th-century Rome ranged from 30 to 80 per 100,000. Today, the intentional homicide rate in all of those countries stands at about 1 per 100,000.[95]

Between 90 percent and 95 percent of all perpetrators of homicide are male. The same is true of 80 percent of murder victims. Eisner notes, "Almost half of all homicides worldwide occurred in just 23 countries that account for 10 per cent of the global population." Unfortunately, medieval levels of violence still afflict countries like El Salvador, Honduras, and South Africa, whose homicide rates

> "As the rule of law, fairer judicial systems, and better policing have spread to more countries around the world, the global homicide rate according to the Institute for Health Metrics and Evaluation has dropped from 6.4 per 100,000 in 1990 to 5.3 per 100,000 in 2017."

are, respectively, 108, 64, and 34 per 100,000. "Without exception societies with high homicide rates suffer from dysfunctional law enforcement and criminal justice systems," notes Eisner. In contrast, about half of the world's population lives in low-homicide societies that account for only 10 percent of all homicides worldwide. As the rule of law, fairer judicial systems, and better policing have spread to more countries around the world, the global homicide rate according to the Institute for Health Metrics and Evaluation has dropped from 6.4 per 100,000 in 1990 to 5.3 per 100,000 in 2017. That's a reduction of 17 percent over a remarkably short period of 26 years, or 0.7 percent per year.[96]

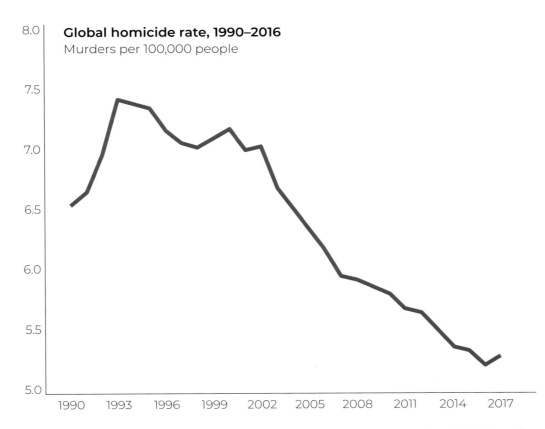

Global homicide rate, 1990–2016
Murders per 100,000 people

Source: Institute for Health Metrics and Evaluation, "GBD Results Tool; Measure: Deaths and DALYs; Age: All Ages; Year: 2017; Cause: Total All Causes; Location: Global; Sex: Both; Metric: Number, Percent, and Rate," Global Burden of Disease Study results, 2018.

CAPITAL PUNISHMENT PLUMMETS

Since time immemorial, people have suffered capital punishment for a plethora of crimes—real and imagined. The Bible's Old Testament, for example, commands the death penalty for murder, kidnapping, attacking or cursing one's parents, sacrificing one's child to Moloch, willful negligence, sorcery, being a medium or spiritist, breaking the Sabbath, sacrificing to idols, blaspheming against God, false prophecy, giving false testimony in a capital case, adultery, incest, rape of a betrothed or married woman, homosexuality, bestiality, prostitution, pretending to be a virgin, and other offenses. As late as the 18th century, the British legal system included 222 capital crimes. The Black Act of 1723

> "As the ideas of the Enlightenment spread, punishment became less gruesome, and the number of capital offenses dwindled."

alone created 50 capital offenses for such crimes as shoplifting and stealing sheep, cattle, and horses.

Types of executions have included beheading, burning, crushing, boiling to death, impaling, hanging, breaking on the wheel, sawing, crucifying, and many others. As the ideas of the Enlightenment spread, punishment became less gruesome, and the number of capital offenses dwindled. In Great Britain alone, the number of capital offenses fell from 222 to 4 in the first half of the 19th century.

Yet the society did not become more chaotic. On the contrary, overall violence decreased. As such, reform-minded governments felt emboldened to go further and abolish the death penalty altogether.

Of the extant states, Venezuela was the first to abolish capital punishment, in 1863.

Other states followed, though it took another century before the abolitionist movement really took off in the 1960s.[97] In 2018, Amnesty International noted, "106 countries (a majority of the world's states) had abolished the death penalty in law for all crimes, and 142 countries (more than two-thirds) had abolished the death penalty in law or practice." Most of the executions took place in China, Iran, Iraq, Saudi Arabia, and Vietnam. Excluding China, which executes thousands of people each year, some 690 executions took place globally in 2018. That number was 31 percent lower than in 2017 and amounts to the lowest number of executions recorded over the past 10 years.[98]

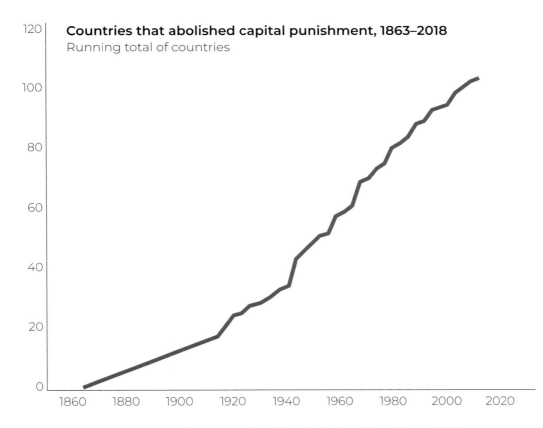

Countries that abolished capital punishment, 1863–2018
Running total of countries

Source: Steven Pinker, personal communication with author (Marian L. Tupy), August 18, 2018.

BATTLE DEATH RATE IS DECLINING

Another measure of the general decline in violence is the global battle death rate per 100,000 people. Researchers associated with the Peace Research Institute Oslo and the SDG16 Data Initiative have documented a steep decline in the rate at which soldiers and civilians were killed in combat in the post–World War II era. The rate of battle deaths per 100,000 people reached a peak of 23 in 1953. By 2016, it had fallen by about 95 percent.[99] The rate of battle deaths rose significantly

> **"The Vietnam War was the first war in which gruesome images of mangled bodies and obliterated villages and cities were broadcast nightly into millions of homes. Since then, televised war reporting has only become more pervasive."**

from a low of about 2 per 100,000 in the late 1950s to approximately 10 per 100,000 in the late 1960s as the Vietnam War heated up. In a 2018 analysis of interstate war trends, two Norwegian mathematicians associated with the Peace Research Institute suggested that the Vietnam War was when the momentum toward a more peaceful world really took hold. Why? Television.[100] The Vietnam War was the first war in which gruesome images of mangled bodies and obliterated villages and cities were broadcast nightly into millions of homes. Since then, televised war reporting has only become more pervasive.

As the war in Southeast Asia ground on, Americans and their allies became less willing to accept high death tolls from conflicts abroad. Other analysts argue that falling fertility rates mean that parents become more protective of the few children they have. One consequence is that low-fertility societies become increasingly averse to war casualties. It is worth noting that most of the current intrastate wars identified by the Council on Foreign Relations' Global Conflict Tracker are occurring in high-fertility countries. One happy result of falling global fertility rates might well be a more peaceful world.

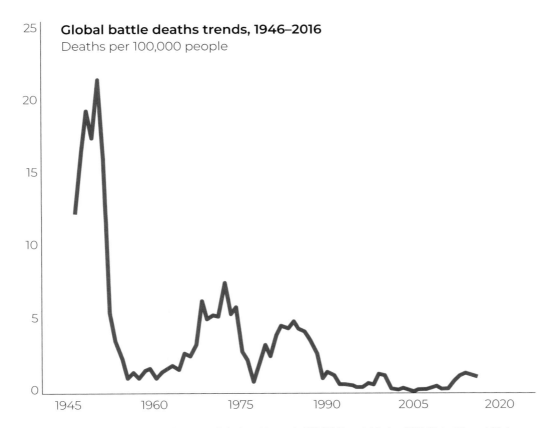

Global battle deaths trends, 1946–2016
Deaths per 100,000 people

Source: UN Sustainable Development Solutions Network, "SDG16 Data Initiative: 2018 Global Report," July 2018, p. 5.

GENOCIDES ARE DISAPPEARING

According to Frank Chalk and Kurt Jonassohn from Concordia University, mass killings of unarmed civilians have "been practiced in all regions of the world and during all periods in history."[101] Some early examples of such massacres include the Athenian destruction of the island of Melos during the Peloponnesian War, the Israelite slaughter of the Midianites during the life of Moses, and the Roman razing of Carthage at the end of the Third Punic War.

In the first half of the 20th century, well-known acts of mass murder included the Turkish pogrom against the Armenians and the German extermination of 6 million Jews. It was in response to the Holocaust that the United Nations Convention on the Prevention and Punishment of the Crime of Genocide outlawed genocide in 1948 and defined it as "acts committed with intent to destroy, in whole or in part, a national, ethnical, racial or religious group."[102]

Genocides, notes Harvard University psychologist Steven Pinker in his 2018 book *Enlightenment Now: The Case for Reason, Science, Humanism, and Progress*, tend to go hand in hand with wars. During World War II, for example, the global death rate among civilians reached 350 per 100,000 per year. Since that time, genocides have become less deadly. The mass murder of unarmed civilians in the second half of the 20th century peaked during the Bangladesh War of Independence in 1971, when the global death rate temporarily rose to

> "It was in response to the Holocaust that the United Nations Convention on the Prevention and Punishment of the Crime of Genocide outlawed genocide in 1948 and defined it as 'acts committed with intent to destroy, in whole or in part, a national, ethnical, racial or religious group.'"

49 people per 100,000. The Cambodian Killing Fields of 1975–1979 are likewise visible on the graph to the right, constituting a mass killing of 2 million individuals. And while the Rwandan genocide of 1994 ranks as probably the worst such episode in recent years, it is undeniable that this event was also of a smaller scale.

Since 2000, mass killings of civilians have become rarer still. The global genocide death rate last peaked at 2 per 100,000 in 2004. Since 2005, it stood at zero. That does not mean that mass murder has disappeared. According to the Uppsala Conflict Data Program, "Intentional attacks on civilians by governments and formally organized armed groups" accounted for 7,088 lost lives in 2017.[103] That said, Pinker is surely right when he writes, "One can never use the word 'fortunately' in connection with the killing of innocents, but the numbers [of civilians killed] in the 21st century are a fraction of those in earlier decades."[104]

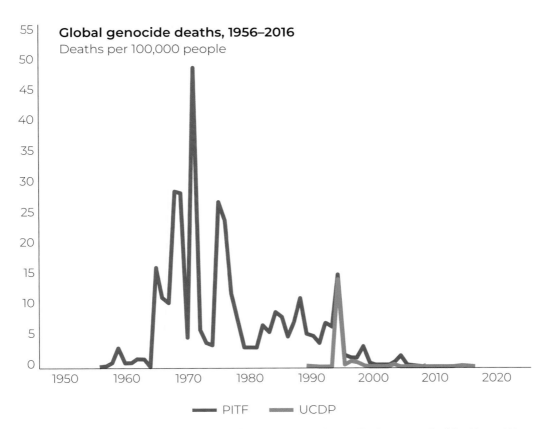

Global genocide deaths, 1956–2016
Deaths per 100,000 people

PITF ■ UCDP

Source: Steven Pinker, "Has the Decline of Violence Reversed since *The Better Angels of Our Nature* Was Written?," 2017.
Note: PITF = Political Instability Task Force; UCDP = Uppsala Conflict Data Program

MILITARY SPENDING RATIO FALLING

In 1960, global spending on the military was 6 percent of world gross domestic product (GDP). By 2017, it had fallen to 2.2 percent. That's a reduction of 63 percent. Traditionally, the Middle East and North Africa had the highest military spending as a share of GDP, which peaked at 12.3 percent in 1991. In 2017, it stood at 5.7 percent. That's a 54 percent decline. Next came North America, which spent 8.4 percent of its GDP on the military in 1962. In 2017, it spent 3 percent—a decline of 64 percent. Military spending in Europe and Central Asia declined from 4.5 percent in 1960 to 1.7 percent in 2017—a reduction of 62 percent.[105]

Military spending in South Asia peaked at 4 percent in 1987. Last year, it stood at 2.5 percent. Sub-Saharan Africa spent the most on the military in 1975 (4 percent). In 2017, that figure stood at a paltry 1.3 percent. Finally, military spending in East Asia and the Pacific peaked at 1.9 percent in 1982. Last year, it stood at 1.7 percent of GDP.

Note that in actual dollars, military spending continues to rise. The Stockholm International Peace Research Institute, for example, estimates that between 1988 and 2017, global military spending rose from $1.424 trillion to $1.686 trillion (figures are in 2016 U.S. dollars).[106] That amounts to an appreciation of 18 percent. Over the same period, however, the world's economy grew from $35.5 trillion to $80 trillion (figures are in 2010 U.S. dollars). That's an increase of 125 percent. If military spending kept pace with economic growth, the world's military expenditures in 2017 would amount to a staggering $3.2 trillion.

> "If military spending kept pace with economic growth, the world's military expenditures in 2017 would amount to a staggering $3.2 trillion."

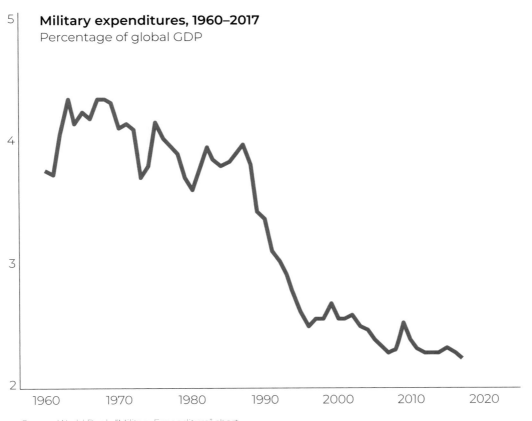

Military expenditures, 1960–2017
Percentage of global GDP

Source: World Bank, "Military Expenditure" chart.
Note: GDP = gross domestic product

ARMIES SHRINK AS A PROPORTION OF POPULATION

In his 2011 book *The Better Angels of Our Nature: Why Violence Has Declined*, Harvard University psychologist Steven Pinker noted that the frequency, duration, and lethality of international wars started to decline after the end of World War II.[107] This process of pacification, which Pinker calls the "Long Peace," accelerated after the Cold War ended in 1989. In 2018, the Council on Foreign Relations Global Conflict Tracker registered no international wars—apart from the "frozen" conflicts between India and Pakistan, and between North and South Korea.[108] As such, the proportion of men and women at arms is at its lowest level since 1989. Armed forces personnel as a share of the global labor force declined from 1.1 percent in 1990 to 0.8 percent in 2016. That's a reduction of 27 percent. The largest decline—from 5.5 to 2.3 percent—took place in the Middle East and North Africa. That's a reduction of 58 percent. Central Asia, Europe, and North America also saw steep declines. The only region that became more militarized was South Asia. The armed forces personnel as a share of the labor force in that region rose from 0.5 percent in 1990 to 0.7 percent in 2016.

In actual numbers, total armed personnel in the world rose from 22.2 million in 1985 to 27.5 million in 2016. That's a 24 percent increase. However, the global population rose from 4.87 billion to 7.63 billion over the same period. That's an increase of 57 percent. Put differently, the number of armed forces personnel has expanded at less than half the rate of population growth. Had the two grown in tandem, the world would have 34.9 million people at arms in 2016.

There is, of course, no guarantee that the Long Peace will endure. That said, humanity is currently enjoying a historically unique period of interstate peace accompanied by a substantial decline in the militarization of our societies.

> "There is, of course, no guarantee that the Long Peace will endure. That said, humanity is currently enjoying a historically unique period of interstate peace accompanied by a substantial decline in the militarization of our societies."

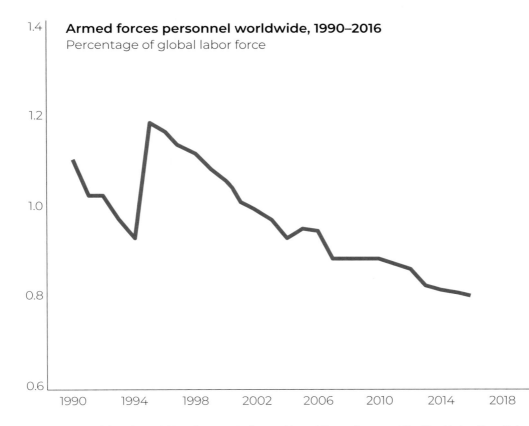

Armed forces personnel worldwide, 1990–2016
Percentage of global labor force

Source: World Bank, *World Development Indicators*, "Armed Forces Personnel (% of Total Labor Force)" chart.

NUCLEAR ARSENALS DWINDLE

On August 6, 1945, the Japanese city of Hiroshima was obliterated by an American uranium bomb called Little Boy. Three days later, a U.S. plutonium bomb called Fat Man flattened a second Japanese city, Nagasaki. Some 200,000 people died as a result of the two explosions.[109] The Japanese Empire surrendered, and World War II came to an end. Once the awesome power of these new weapons was revealed, a global nuclear arms race ensued. The Soviet Union got its first bomb in 1949, Great Britain in 1953, China and France

> **"The end of the ideological conflict between the two superpowers accounts for much of the reduced number of nuclear warheads, along with the adoption of various arms limitation treaties."**

in 1964, and Israel in 1967. Those were the principal nuclear powers during the Cold War.

At the height of the Cold War in 1986, the nations of the world possessed 64,449 nuclear warheads capable of destroying our planet many times over. With 40,159 warheads, the USSR led the way. The United States was the runner up with 23,317 warheads. Since the end of the Cold War in 1991, the number of nuclear powers actually increased, as India, Pakistan, and North Korea joined the club. But in contrast, the number of warheads declined to 9,305 in 2018—an 86 percent reduction.

The end of the ideological conflict between the two superpowers accounts for much of the reduced number of nuclear warheads, along with the adoption of various arms limitation

treaties. Moreover, nuclear weapons are expensive to develop, build, maintain, and protect. The United States, for example, is estimated to have spent $11.6 trillion (in 2018 U.S. dollars) on its nuclear arsenal between 1940 and 2005.[110] Finally, nuclear powers have realized that relatively few nuclear weapons are necessary to deter their enemies.

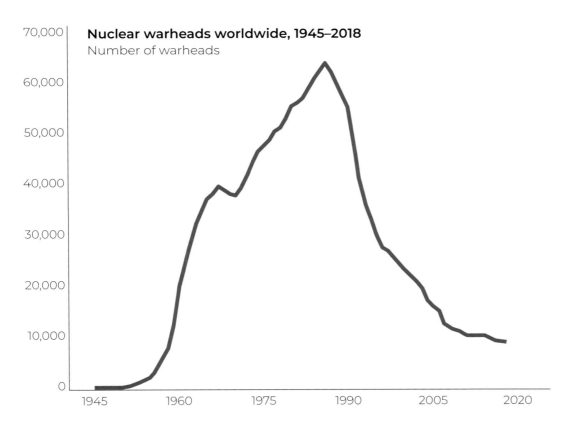

Nuclear warheads worldwide, 1945–2018
Number of warheads

Source: Hans M. Kristensen and Robert S. Norris, "Status of World Nuclear Forces," Federation of American Scientists, November 21, 2018.

TREND 42

WORKING LESS FOR MORE

Based on their observations of extant hunter-gatherer societies, scholars estimate that our foraging ancestors worked anywhere between 2.8 hours and 7.6 hours per day.[111] Once they secured their food for the day, they stopped. The foragers' workload was comparatively low, but so was their standard of living. Our ancestors' wealth was limited to the weight of the possessions they could carry on their backs from one location to the next.

About 12,000 years ago, people started to settle down, cultivate crops, and domesticate animals. The total number of hours worked rose, but people

> **"The overall number of hours worked has declined in tandem with increasing prosperity. Plainly put, the richer the country, the less people work."**

were willing to sacrifice free time in exchange for a more stable food supply. Since artificial lighting was prohibitively expensive, daylight regulated the amount of work that could be done. In summer, most people worked between 6 and 10 hours in the fields and an additional 3 hours at home. In winter, daylight limited the total number of work hours to 8.

By 1830, the workweek in the industrializing West averaged about 70 hours, Sundays excluded, or 11.6 hours of work per day. By 1890, that fell to 60 hours per week, or 10 hours per day. Thirty years later, the workweek in advanced societies stood at 50 hours, or 8.3 hours per day. Today, people in advanced societies work fewer than 40 hours per week. That still amounts to roughly 8 hours per day, because workers typically don't work on Saturdays.

The overall number of hours worked has declined in tandem with increasing prosperity. Plainly put, the richer the country, the less people work. Data for developing countries are difficult to come by, but the population-adjusted total annual number of hours worked in 81 developed countries and their dependencies declined from 2,123 in 1950 to 1,732 in 2017.[112] That's a decrease of 18.4 percent. Based on the available data, Germans worked the fewest hours (1,347) and Singaporeans worked the most hours (2,237).

With 1,763 work-hours per year, the United States was squarely in the middle of the pack in 2017.[113]

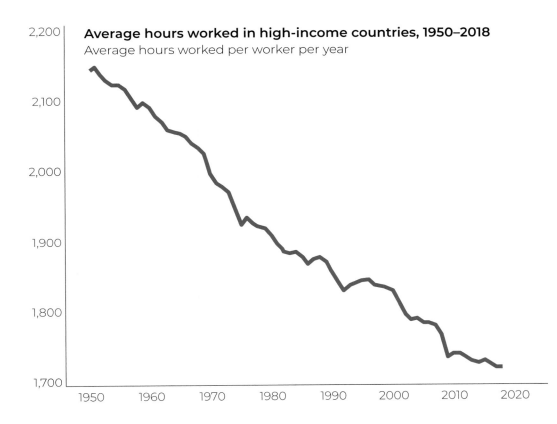

Average hours worked in high-income countries, 1950–2018
Average hours worked per worker per year

Source: Authors' calculation based on data from the Conference Board, Total Economy Database—Key
Findings, April 2019.

WORK GROWS SAFER

All economic activity involves some degree of physical risk. Credible data on work injuries and fatalities among our agrarian ancestors are difficult to come by. Yet agricultural work must have been quite unappealing, considering that so many people in the early 19th century preferred factory work over farm work.

Even today, notes the U.S. Department of Labor, agriculture "ranks among the most dangerous industries." In 2011, the "fatality rate for agricultural workers was 7 times higher than the fatality rate for all workers in private

> **"Credible data on work injuries and fatalities among our agrarian ancestors are difficult to come by. Yet agricultural work must have been quite unappealing, considering that so many people in the early 19th century preferred factory work over farm work."**

industry; agricultural workers had a fatality rate of 24.9 deaths per 100,000, while the fatality rate for all workers was 3.5."[114] Likewise, the Workplace Safety and Health (WSH) Institute in Singapore found that global fatality rates per 100,000 employees in agriculture ranged from 7.8 deaths in high-income countries to 27.5 deaths in the Southeast Asia and Western Pacific regions in 2014. Manufacturing deaths ranged from 3.8 in high-income countries to 21.1 in Africa.[115]

By modern standards, working conditions in mines and factories during the first 100 years of the Industrial Revolution were appalling. As U.S. President Benjamin Harrison put it in 1892, "American workmen are subjected to peril of life and limb as great as a soldier in time of war."[116] In the United States, estimates Harvard University psychologist Steven Pinker, 61 per 100,000 workers died in work-related accidents as late as 1913. That number fell to 3.2 in 2015. That's a

95 percent reduction.[117] A similarly encouraging trend applies globally. According to the WSH Institute estimates, 16.4 workers per 100,000 employees died worldwide in 1998. By 2014 that number fell to 11.3. That's a 31 percent reduction over a remarkably short period of 16 years. Put differently, workplace fatalities seem to be falling by almost 2 percentage points each year.[118]

What accounts for those improvements? Labor union activism, including strikes and protests, has been traditionally credited with making the workplace safer. The massive economic expansion in the second half of the 19th century also tightened the labor market, empowering workers to gravitate toward more generous employers. Only after a critical mass of workers achieved more tolerable working conditions did more general workplace regulations become imaginable and, more importantly, economically sustainable.

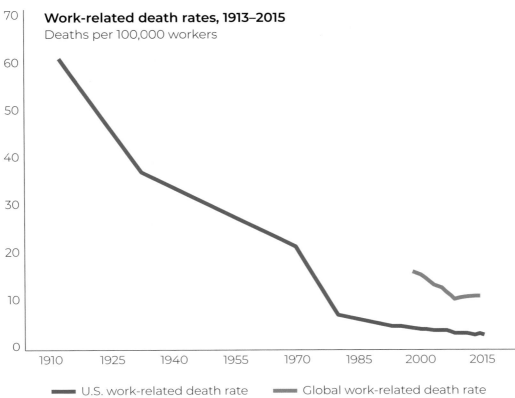

Work-related death rates, 1913–2015
Deaths per 100,000 workers

—— U.S. work-related death rate   —— Global work-related death rate

Sources: Steven Pinker, personal communication with author (Marian L. Tupy), August 13, 2018; and Päivi Hämäläinen, Jukka Takala, and Tan Boon Kiat, *Global Estimates of Occupational Accidents and Work-Related Illnesses* (Singapore: Workplace Safety and Health Institute, 2017).

CHILDREN LABOR LESS

Child labor was once ubiquitous. Before the mechanization of agriculture, which increased farm productivity, there were no "food surpluses" to sustain idle hands—including those of children. "The survival of the family demanded that everybody contributed," writes Johan Norberg in his 2016 book *Progress: Ten Reasons to Look Forward to the Future*. "It was common for working-class children to start working from seven years of age."[119]

As agricultural productivity increased, people no longer had to stay on the farm and grow their food. They moved to towns and cities in search of a better life. At first, living conditions were dire, with many children working in mines and factories. By the middle of the 19th century, however, working conditions started to improve. Economic expansion led to an increased competition for labor, and wages grew. That, in turn, enabled more parents to forgo their children's labor and send them to school instead.

Between 1851 and 1911, the share of British working boys and girls between the ages of 10 and 14 dropped from 37 percent and 20 percent, respectively, to 18 percent and 10 percent. In the United States, the share of working 10- to 13-year-olds fell from 12 percent in 1890 to 2.5 percent in 1930.[120]

According to the International Labour Organization, child laborers as a proportion of all children ages 5 to 17 dropped globally from 16 percent in 2000 to 9.6 percent in 2016. That year, 19.6 percent of children worked in Africa, 7.4 percent in Asia and the Pacific, 5.3 percent in the Americas, 4.1 percent in Europe and Central Asia, and 2.9 percent in the Arab states.

The total number of child laborers fell from 246 million in 2000 to 152 million in 2016. Almost half of child laborers in 2016 were in Africa (72.1 million), 62.1 million were in Asia and the Pacific, 10.7 million were in the Americas, 5.5 million were in Europe and Central Asia, and 1.2 million were in the Arab States. Agriculture accounted for 71 percent of child laborers, services for 17 percent, and industry for 12 percent. In spite of continued population growth, the International Labour Organization expects that by 2025 the total number of child laborers will decline to between 121 million and 88 million.

> **"Before the mechanization of agriculture, which increased farm productivity, there were no 'food surpluses' to sustain idle hands—including those of children."**

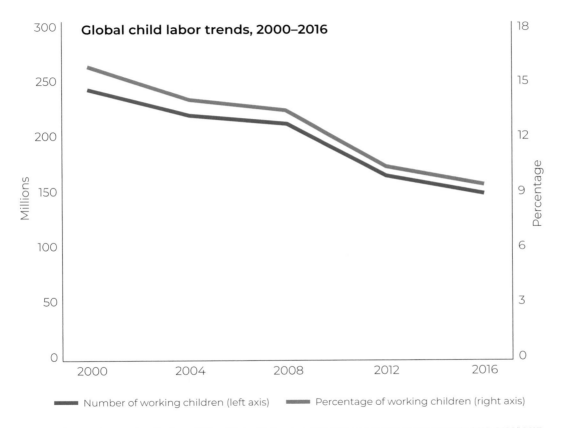

Global child labor trends, 2000–2016

— Number of working children (left axis)　　— Percentage of working children (right axis)

Source: International Labour Office, "Global Estimates of Child Labour: Results and Trends, 2012–2016," 2017.

THE CHANGING NATURE OF WORK

Before the Industrial Revolution, between 80 percent and 90 percent of the world's population worked in agriculture. At the start of the 19th century, people in Western Europe and North America began to move into manufacturing jobs en masse. Factory jobs have been criticized by philosophers like Karl Marx, lampooned by comedians like Charlie Chaplin, and bemoaned by poets like William Blake.

By and large, people moved from farm work to factory work in the cities willingly, for the latter provided higher wages, greater independence, and cultural stimulation. The share of the U.S. workforce employed on farms fell from 90 percent in 1790 to less than 2 percent today.[121] The decline in agricultural employment still continues elsewhere. Between 1991 and 2018, agricultural employment fell from 44 percent to 28 percent globally. Only in very poor countries, such as Bhutan and Zimbabwe, does agriculture continue to employ over 50 percent of laborers.[122]

In the United States, the manufacturing sector employed just 15 percent of the workforce in 1880.[123] Manufacturing employment peaked at 38 percent in 1944. By 2019, it fell to 8.5 percent.[124] Conversely, the share of workers employed in the service sector rose from 31 percent in 1900 to 78 percent in 1999.[125] In 2016, it stood at 81 percent.[126] Similar trends can be observed in other advanced economies, such as Germany, Japan, and the United Kingdom.

Meanwhile, manufacturing jobs have grown in countries that embraced industrialization in more recent decades. Between 1991 and 2018, for example, industrial employment rose from 14 percent to 21 percent in Bangladesh, from 22 percent to 29 percent in China, from 15 percent to 25 percent in India, and from 12 percent to 26 percent in Vietnam.[127]

"The service sector will play an increasingly prominent part in their economic development."

History suggests that, as these rapidly industrializing countries become richer, the service sector will play an increasingly prominent part in their economic development.

Are these employment trends cause for worry? Far from it. The service sector consists of jobs in the information sector, investment services, technical and scientific services, healthcare, and social assistance services, as well as in arts, entertainment, and recreation. Most of these jobs are less physically arduous, more intellectually stimulating, and better paid than either agricultural or manufacturing jobs. They are also less dangerous. In 2014, global fatality rates per 100,000 employees in agriculture ranged from 7.8 deaths in high-income countries to 27.5 deaths in Southeast Asia and the Western Pacific. In manufacturing, the range was from 3.8 in high-income countries to 21.1 in Africa. The range for the service sector was from 1.5 in high-income countries to 17.7 in Africa.[128]

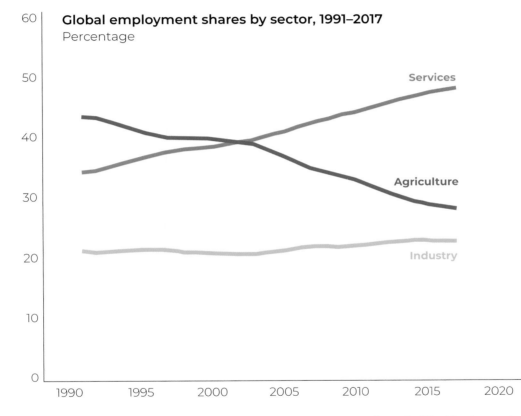

Global employment shares by sector, 1991–2017
Percentage

Services

Agriculture

Industry

Sources: World Bank, *World Development Indicators*, "Employment in Industry (% of Total Employment) (Modeled International Labour Organization Estimate)" chart; "Employment in Agriculture (% of Total Employment) (Modeled ILO Estimate)" chart; and "Employment in Service (% of Total Employment) (Modeled ILO Estimate)" chart.

TREND 46

THE WAGE GAP BETWEEN MEN AND WOMEN IS NARROWING

Jonathan Haidt, a psychologist working at New York University, has noted that social values change with income. In preindustrial societies, life is difficult and unpredictable. People tend to emphasize traditional and survival values, such as family, duty, and prayer. As societies grow richer, life becomes safer. "Fading existential pressures open people's minds, making them prioritize freedom over security. The generation raised with these 'open minds' and 'expressive values' starts caring about women's rights. They start expecting more out of life than their parents did."[129]

The ideal of gender equality began to emerge during the Enlightenment in the 18th century. The practice of gender equality, however, had to wait until women secured for themselves independent sources of income. That they initially did by working in factories during the Industrial Revolution. Not surprisingly, gender wage equality has reached its apex in countries that developed first.

According to the World Economic Forum's report *The Global Gender Gap Index 2018*, Western Europe, North America, and Eastern Europe and Central Asia were the regions closest to gender wage parity, whereas the Middle East and North Africa, South Asia, and Sub-Saharan Africa were the regions furthest from gender wage parity.[130] The World Economic Forum provides only a snapshot of global wage disparities in 2018. For a longitudinal study of wage differences between men and women, consider data from the Organisation for Economic Co-operation and Development. The OECD defines the gender wage gap as the "difference between median earnings of men and women relative to median earnings of men."[131] The OECD includes 36 highly developed countries. There, the average wage gap declined from 19 percent in 1995 to 14 percent in 2016. That year, Romania had the lowest wage gap of 1.5 percent, whereas South Korea had the highest wage gap of 35 percent.[132] The OECD wage gap does not tell the full story of women's empowerment. It is worth noting that once the relevant differences between men and women in the choice of occupations, college majors, and length of time in the workplace are adjusted for, the wage gap in many highly developed nations narrows to the point of insignificance.[133]

> "The ideal of gender equality began to emerge during the Enlightenment in the 18th century. The practice of gender equality, however, had to wait until women secured for themselves independent sources of income."

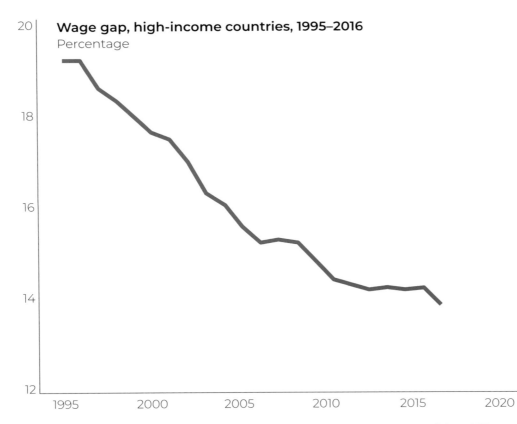

Wage gap, high-income countries, 1995–2016
Percentage

Source: Organisation for Economic Co-operation and Development, "Gender Wage Gap" chart, 2019.

UNIVERSAL EMANCIPATION

Slavery can be traced back to Sumer, a Middle Eastern civilization that flourished between 4500 BCE and 1900 BCE. Before the age of steam, humanity depended on energy produced primarily by people and animals. An extra pair of hands always welcome in the fields, and conquered people who weren't killed were frequently put to work as slaves.

Slavery existed in ancient Egypt, India, Greece, China, Rome, and pre-Columbian America. The Arab slave trade took off during the Muslim conquests of the Middle Ages. The word "slave" probably derives from the Late Latin word *sclavus*, which in turn denotes the Slavic peoples of Central and Eastern Europe who were enslaved by the Ottoman Turks.

Slavery in the Caribbean and the southeastern United States, which was practiced between the 16th and 19th centuries CE, saw millions of Africans brought to the New World for that very purpose. Yet slavery among African tribes, especially those in West Africa, was also common and persisted until very recently. In fact, Mauritania became the last country to outlaw slavery in 1981. In spite of the ban, slavery continued to be practiced, however. Consequently, the

government of Mauritania criminalized the practice of enslavement in 2007.[134] As chattel slavery disappeared, our definition of slavery has expanded to include such practices as forced labor, sexual slavery, and debt bondage. The elimination of such servitude will be the challenge of the 21st century. But let's not lose sight of the moral progress humanity has made by eliminating the ancient institution of chattel slavery and making it an anathema throughout the world.

> "As chattel slavery disappeared, our definition of slavery has expanded to include such practices as forced labor, sexual slavery, and debt bondage."

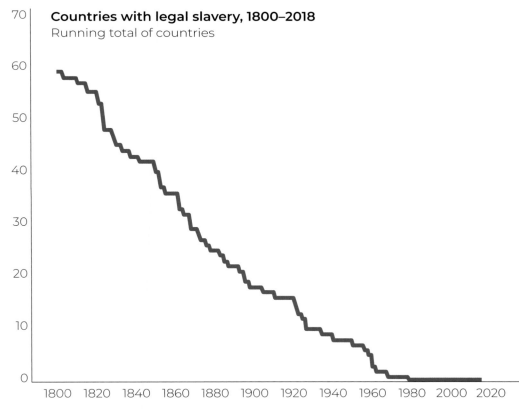

Countries with legal slavery, 1800–2018
Running total of countries

Source: Steven Pinker, personal communication with author (Marian L. Tupy), July 16, 2018.

NATURAL RESOURCE TRENDS

TREND 48
PEAK FARMLAND

Considering that agriculture is the most expansive and intensive way in which people transform natural landscapes, the good news is that the amount of land globally devoted to food production may soon begin falling as population growth slows and agricultural productivity increases. "We believe that projecting conservative values for population, affluence, consumers, and technology shows humanity peaking in the use of farmland," argues Jesse Ausubel, director of the Program for the Human Environment at Rockefeller University, and his colleagues in their 2013 article "Peak Farmland and the Prospect for Land Sparing."

Crops were planted on 1.371 billion hectares (3.387 billion acres) globally in 1961. That rose to 1.533 billion hectares (3.788 billion acres) in 2009. Ausubel and his coauthors project a return to 1.385 billion hectares (3.422 billion acres) in 2060, thus restoring at least 146 million hectares (360 million acres)

to nature.[135] This is an area two and a half times that of France, or the size of 10 Iowas. Although cropland has continued to expand slowly since 2009, the UN Food and Agriculture Organization reports that land devoted to agriculture (including pastures) peaked in 2000 at 4.915 billion hectares (12.15 billion acres) and had fallen to 4.828 billion hectares (11.93 billion acres) by 2017.[136] This human withdrawal from the landscape is the likely prelude to a vast ecological restoration over the course of this century.

"Considering that agriculture is the most expansive and intensive way in which people transform natural landscapes, the good news is that the amount of land globally devoted to food production may soon begin falling as population growth slows and agricultural productivity increases."

Under a slightly more optimistic scenario in which people choose to eat somewhat less meat, and in which the demand for biofuels falls, Ausubel and his colleagues project that an additional 256 million hectares (633 million acres) would be spared from the plow. That would mean nearly 400 million hectares (988 million acres) restored to nature by 2060, an area almost twice the size of the United States east of the Mississippi River. The researchers conclude, "Now we are confident that we stand on the peak of cropland use, gazing at a wide expanse of land that will be spared for Nature."[137]

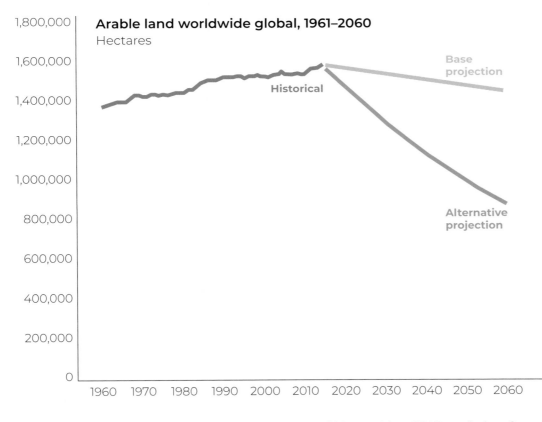

Arable land worldwide global, 1961–2060
Hectares

Historical

Base projection

Alternative projection

Source: Jesse H. Ausubel, "Peak Farmland and Potatoes" (plenary address, 2014 Potato Business Summit of the United Potato Growers of America, San Antonio, TX, January 8, 2014), p. 6.

CONSERVING MORE LAND AND SEA

Countries began formally setting aside landscapes as protected parks and nature preserves in the late 19th century. The Yosemite Valley was dedicated in 1864 as a California state park, whereas Yellowstone National Park was established as the world's first national park in 1872.

The UN Convention on Biological Diversity (CBD)—which was finalized in 1992 and has now been signed by 168 countries—aims to protect the world's wildlife and wildlands. Under the CBD, a protected area is broadly characterized as "a geographically defined area, which is designated or regulated and managed to achieve specific conservation objectives." In 2010, signatories to the CBD agreed to the goal of setting aside at least 17 percent of terrestrial and inland waters, and 10 percent of coastal and marine areas, as protected areas by 2020.

The World Database on Protected Areas reported as of 2018 that about 15 percent of the earth's land surface is now covered by protected areas, an expanse amounting to over 20 million square kilometers (7.7 million square miles). That area is nearly double the size of the entire United States.[138]

Marine protected areas now account for nearly 7 percent of the global ocean, which amounts to over 26 million square kilometers (10 million square miles). That area is more than double the size of South America. Globally, that totals to 46 million square kilometers of protected areas (17.8 million square miles)[139]—just a bit over the size of all of Asia.

Humanity is well on the way toward achieving the goal of setting aside 59 million square kilometers (nearly 23 million square miles) of land and sea for nature by 2020.

> "Humanity is well on the way toward achieving the goal of setting aside 59 million square kilometers (nearly 23 million square miles) of land and sea for nature by 2020."

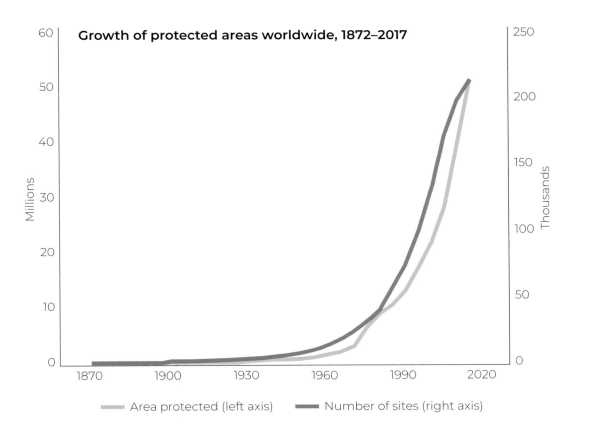

Growth of protected areas worldwide, 1872–2017

Area protected (left axis) ━━━ Number of sites (right axis)

Sources: For 1872–2003 data, see S. Chape et al., "Measuring the Extent and Effectiveness of Protected Areas as an Indicator for Meeting Global Biodiversity Targets," *Phil. Trans. R. Soc. B 360* (2005): 450, figure 1; and UN Environment Programme; Protected Planet, World Database on Protected Areas.

DECARBONIZING THE ECONOMY

Over the past two centuries, the size of the world's economy has increased more than a hundredfold. That expansion was powered by fossil fuels, the burning of which helped raise the level of carbon dioxide (CO_2) in the atmosphere from 0.0284 percent in 1820 to 0.0407 percent in 2017. Many scientists worry that this increase in atmospheric CO_2 could lead to deleterious long-term consequences, including runaway global warming. We are some years away from seeing dependable and financially viable sources of energy that are completely harmless to the environment. In the meantime, economic growth and, consequently, people's rising standards of living, will continue to require fossil fuels. The good news is that production processes are becoming more environmentally friendly throughout much of the world.

The World Bank estimates that the United States produces roughly 24 percent of the world's wealth. The European Union produces 22 percent, China 15 percent, Japan 6 percent, and Germany, if considered independently of the EU, 5 percent. Now consider CO_2 emissions per dollar of gross domestic product. In 1960, the United States emitted 0.94 kilograms of CO_2 per dollar of output. By 2014, that number fell to 0.32. That's a reduction of 66 percent. The EU has reduced its CO_2 emissions per dollar of output from 0.57 to 0.19 kilograms. That's a reduction of 68 percent. After China abandoned its inefficient communist system of production, its CO_2 emissions per dollar of output fell from 5 kilograms in 1978 to 1.24 kilograms in 2014—a reduction of 75 percent. Japanese emissions fell from 0.3 kilograms in 1960 to 0.2 kilograms in 2014, or 33 percent. Finally, German emissions fell from 0.34 kilograms in 1991 to 0.2 kilograms in 2017, or 41 percent.[140] This downward trend in emissions per dollar is largely the result of businesses' constant efforts to reduce their energy costs. That's one of the reasons why global CO_2 emissions per dollar of output declined from 0.84 kilograms in 1960 to 0.5 kilograms in 2014, or 41 percent. Moreover, technological improvements in production processes are likely to continue to reduce fuel consumption per dollar of output and, consequently, lower CO_2 emissions even further. Reductions in absolute quantities of CO_2 have not yet materialized outside of economic recessions, but this type of progress is at least a distinct step in a positive direction.

> "This downward trend in emissions per dollar is largely the result of businesses' constant efforts to reduce their energy costs."

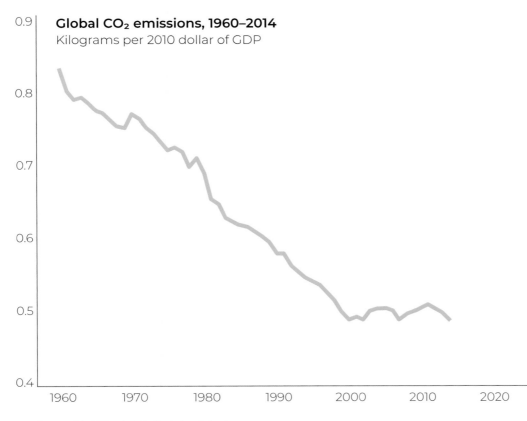

Global CO$_2$ emissions, 1960–2014
Kilograms per 2010 dollar of GDP

Source: World Bank, "CO$_2$ Emissions" chart.
Note: GDP = gross domestic product

NO PEAK OIL

As reliance on petroleum as a source of energy grew over the past century and a half, predictions that humanity was about to run out of its limited supply multiplied. For example, David White of the U.S. Geological Survey warned in 1919 that world oil production would peak in just nine years. Nearly a century later, Princeton University geologist Ken Deffeyes predicted that the peak of global oil production would occur on Thanksgiving Day 2005.[141]

Instead, global production of crude oil has been steadily rising, from an average of approximately 32 million barrels per day in 1965 to 95 million in 2018.[142] Predictions that world reserves were about to peak and begin declining have also proved wrong. In the wake of the 1970s oil crises, global proven reserves in 1980 were estimated at 684 billion barrels.[143] That year, the world was pumping 23 billion barrels of crude oil annually. By implication, only 30 years of oil was left to be extracted.

Instead of running out, however, the world has pumped 983 billion barrels of oil since 1980.[144] Meanwhile, proven reserves of crude oil have nearly tripled, to 1.7 trillion barrels. In 2017, the world produced 35 billion barrels of oil. At that rate, humanity would run out of oil in 50 years.

> **"Predictions that world reserves were about to peak and begin declining have also proved wrong."**

In 2000, Saudi Arabian oil minister Ahmed Zaki Yamani famously declared, "The Stone Age came to an end not because we had a lack of stones, and the oil age will come to an end not because we have a lack of oil."[145] That dictum is looking prescient. Some researchers—including those at the Oxford Institute for Energy Studies—have recently shifted from predicting peak *supply* of oil to instead now forecasting peak *demand* for petroleum sometime in the next 20 to 30 years.

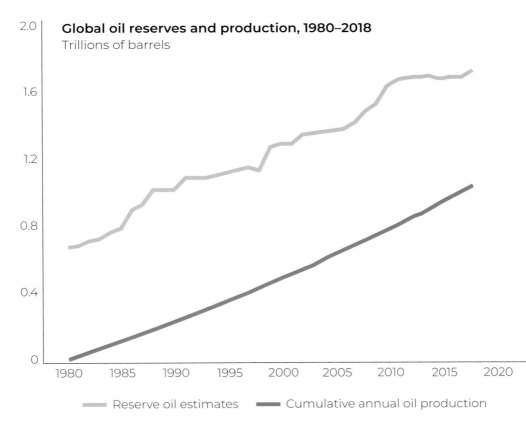

Global oil reserves and production, 1980–2018
Trillions of barrels

Reserve oil estimates — Cumulative annual oil production

Sources: BP plc, "Statistical Review of World Energy 2019," June 2019; U.S. Energy Information Administration, International data, "Petroleum and Other Liquids."

RISING NATURAL GAS RESERVES

The energy crisis of the 1970s also featured severe shortages of natural gas in the United States. The upshot was that during the winter months of several years in the mid-1970s, many factories and schools were ordered closed to ensure adequate supplies for home heating. To ameliorate the shortage, the federal government banned the burning of natural gas to produce electricity in 1978 and approved the construction of 20 massive plants to turn coal into natural gas in 1980.

Over the past 50 years, further exploration and the development of new production technologies, like fracking, have boosted global proven reserves of natural gas considerably. World proven reserves of natural gas have risen from an estimated 73.2 billion cubic meters (2,586 trillion cubic feet) in 1980 to 203.2 trillion cubic meters (7,177 trillion cubic feet) in 2019. In 1980, the world produced about 1.4 trillion cubic meters (50 trillion cubic feet) of natural gas. By 2017, annual global production of natural gas had risen to nearly 3.7 trillion cubic meters (130 trillion cubic feet).

U.S. production hovered around 500 billion cubic meters (18 trillion cubic feet) annually until the fracking revolution unlocked supplies of shale gas in the past 10 years. In 2018, the U.S. produced 925 billion cubic meters (32.7 trillion cubic feet) of natural gas.

"To ameliorate the shortage, the federal government banned the burning of natural gas to produce electricity in 1978 and approved the construction of 20 massive plants to turn coal into natural gas in 1980."

Natural gas is no longer banned from being burned to generate electricity. Consequently, cheap abundant natural gas has now displaced coal as the chief fuel for generating electricity in the United States. That's good, because burning natural gas produces less air pollution, including about half the carbon dioxide that burning coal does.

At current rates of production, the world's proven reserves of natural gas would last more than 54 years.

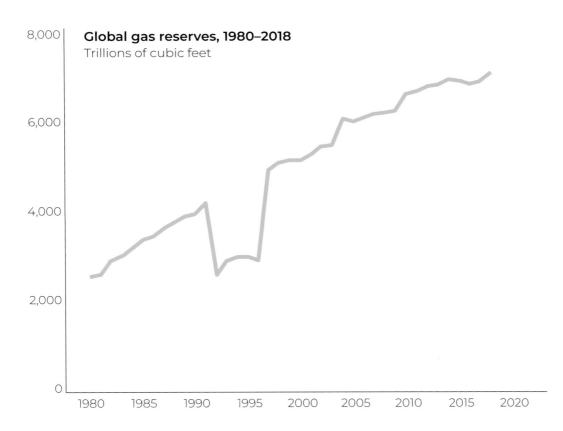

Global gas reserves, 1980–2018
Trillions of cubic feet

Source: U.S. Energy Information Administration, International data, "Natural Gas."

USING WATER MORE EFFICIENTLY

Known renewable water reserves per person have declined from 55,270 cubic meters (1.95 million cubic feet) to 19,248 cubic meters (0.68 million cubic feet) between 1962 and 2014. According to the UN Food and Agriculture Organization: "69 percent of the world's freshwater withdrawals are committed to agriculture. The industrial sector accounts for 19 percent while only 12 percent of water withdrawals are destined for households and municipal use."[146]

Greater efficiencies in agriculture, therefore, are likely to have the greatest effect on the preservation of freshwater supplies. Luckily, precision agriculture—which combines drip and variable-rate irrigation, Global Positioning System technology, automation, and computer monitoring—can deliver the right amount of water to individual plants, thus limiting waste and runoff. Israel, one of the driest places on Earth, has used technological breakthroughs to become an exporter of agricultural products, including tomatoes, cucumbers, zucchini, and watermelons.

Israel has also built innovative water treatment systems, which "recapture 86 percent of the water that goes down the drain and use it for irrigation—vastly more than the second-most-efficient country in the world, Spain, which recycles 19 percent."[147] Another Israeli innovation is a much-improved process of desalination, which makes fresh water consumed by Israeli households 48 percent cheaper than that consumed by the people of Los Angeles. That's particularly important, considering that oceans cover 71 percent of Earth's surface. If scientists can combine desalination with environmentally friendly sources of energy, such as solar panels, in a cost-

> **"Israel has also built innovative water treatment systems, which 'recapture 86 percent of the water that goes down the drain and use it for irrigation—vastly more than the second-most-efficient country in the world, Spain, which recycles 19 percent.'"**

efficient way, freshwater supplies will become limitless.

Finally, it is important to remember that water, like energy, is an input in the process of production. That is to say, water costs money. It is, therefore, in the interest of water-intensive industries to limit their water use. Luckily that is precisely what is happening. Global data are difficult to come by, but consider the five largest economies that together account for more than 50 percent of the world's economic output.

The World Bank estimates that the United States increased its water productivity—or inflation-adjusted dollars of gross domestic product per cubic meter (i.e., 35.3147 cubic feet) of fresh water withdrawn—from $13 in 1980 to $36 in 2010; China from $0.80 in 1980 to $15 in 2015; Japan from $34 in 1980 to $67 in 2009; Germany from $58 in 1991 to $104 in 2010; and the United Kingdom from $91 in 1980 to $314 in 2012.[148]

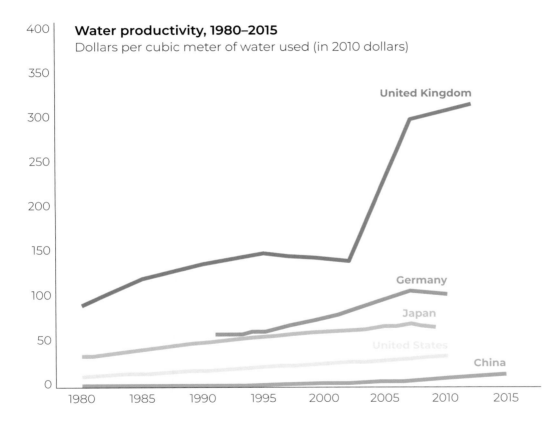

Water productivity, 1980–2015
Dollars per cubic meter of water used (in 2010 dollars)

United Kingdom

Germany

Japan

United States

China

Source: World Bank, "Water Productivity, Total (Constant 2010 US$ GDP per Cubic Meter of Total Freshwater Withdrawal" chart.

PRODUCING MORE WITH LESS

"Dematerialization" refers to the process of declining consumption of material and energy per unit of gross domestic product. That makes economic sense, since spending less on inputs can swell profit margins and make outputs cheaper and, therefore, more competitive.

And dematerialization is good for the environment. "If consumers dematerialize their intensity of use of goods and technicians produce the goods with a lower intensity of impact, people can grow in numbers and affluence without a proportionally greater environmental impact," explain Jesse Ausubel from Rockefeller University and Paul E. Waggoner from the Connecticut Agricultural Experiment Station in a 2008 article in the *Proceedings of the National Academy of Sciences*.[149]

Dematerialization is welcome news for those who worry about the availability of resources for a growing world population. Dematerialization will enable future generations to be better stewards of our planet while continuing to enjoy ever-improving goods and services.

The dematerialization manifested in a smartphone is a good example. The product combines functions that

> **"'Dematerialization' refers to the process of declining consumption of material and energy per unit of gross domestic product. That makes economic sense, since spending less on inputs can swell profit margins and make outputs cheaper and, therefore, more competitive."**

previously required myriad separate devices, including a telephone, camera, radio, television, alarm clock, newspaper, photo album, voice recorder, maps, compass, and more. In 2018, a team of 21 researchers led by Arnulf Grubler from the International Institute for Applied Systems Analysis in Austria estimated the "savings from device convergence on smartphones . . . for materials use (device weight) and for its associated embodied energy use." They found that smartphones can reduce material use by a factor of 300. They can reduce power use by a factor of 100 and standby energy use by a factor of 30.[150]

Resource use and digital convergence

1706 kWh	Embodied energy	75 kWh
449 watts	Power	5 watts
72 watts	Standby energy use	2.5 watts
26 kg	Weight	0.1 kg

Source: Arnulf Grubler et al., "A Low Energy Demand Scenario for Meeting the 1.5 °C Target and Sustainable Development Goals without Negative Emission Technologies," *Nature Energy* 3, no. 1 (2018): 515–27.

FARM TRENDS

TREND 55
HUNGER RETREATS

According to the UN Food and Agriculture Organization (FAO), the prevalence of undernourishment in the world fell from 37 percent of the total population in 1969–1971 to 14.8 percent in 2000, reaching a low of 10.6 in 2015 before ticking up to 10.8 in 2018. The FAO defines the "prevalence of undernourishment" as "an estimate of the proportion of the population whose habitual food consumption is insufficient to provide the dietary energy levels that are required to maintain a normal active and healthy life." Famines caused by drought, floods, pests, and conflict have collapsed whole civilizations and killed hundreds of millions of people over the course of human history. In the 20th century, the biggest famines were caused by communist regimes in the Soviet Union and mainland China. Soviet dictator Josef Stalin's famines killed up to 10 million people,[151] and China's despot Mao Zedong starved 45 million between 1958 and 1962.[152]

> "War and political violence are still major causes of hunger around the world. The outbreaks of conflict and insurgencies in countries like Afghanistan, Nigeria, Somalia, South Sudan, Syria, and Yemen are largely responsible for the recent uptick in the rate of global undernourishment."

In the 21st century, war and political violence are still major causes of hunger around the world. The outbreaks of conflict and insurgencies in countries like Afghanistan, Nigeria, Somalia, South Sudan, Syria, and Yemen are largely responsible for the recent uptick in the rate of global undernourishment. In other words, famines have disappeared outside of war zones. Much progress has been made, and the specter of famine no longer haunts the vast majority of humankind.

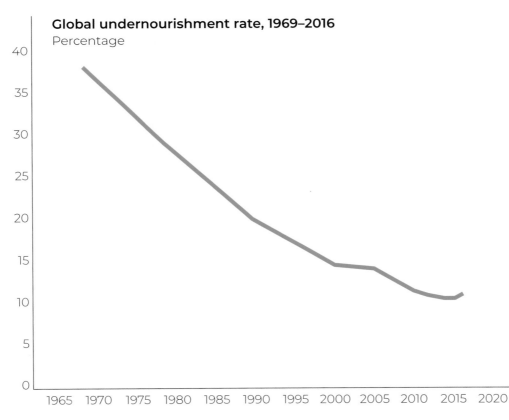

Global undernourishment rate, 1969–2016
Percentage

Sources: For 1969–2005 data, see Food and Agriculture Organization of the United Nations (FAO), "Global Hunger Declining but Still Unacceptably High," Economic and Social Development Department, September 2010, p. 1, figure 2; and for 2005–2016 data, see FAO, "Hunger and Food Insecurity."

GRAIN CORNUCOPIA

More than 50 percent of humanity's daily caloric intake comes directly from cereal grain consumption. Rice contributes about 21 percent of the world's per capita caloric intake. Wheat is a close second, directly providing about 20 percent of world per capita calories. About one-third of cereal grain production (particularly corn, barley, sorghum, and oats) also goes into livestock feed, thus indirectly contributing to human nutrition. After rice and wheat, potatoes are the third-most-important food crop in the world; current global production of potatoes is about 380 million metric tons grown on about 19 million hectares (47 million acres).[153]

In 1961, the world's farmers harvested 735 million metric tons of grains, providing an average of 247 kilograms (545 pounds) for each of the globe's 3 billion people. By 2017, world grain production had nearly quadrupled to 2.98 billion metric tons, affording an average of 380 kilograms (838 pounds) for each of the world's 7.5 billion people

---

> **"About one-third of cereal grain production (particularly corn, barley, sorghum, and oats) also goes into livestock feed, thus indirectly contributing to human nutrition."**

today.[154] This massive increase in grain production took place even though the amount of land used to cultivate food crops only rose from 1.38 billion hectares (3.4 billion acres) in 1961 to 1.59 billion hectares (3.9 billion acres) in 2016.[155] What about the future? Since the 1960s, the annual world population growth rate has decelerated, dropping from 2.1 percent to about 1 percent now, and it is expected to fall further to 0.5 percent by 2050. Meanwhile, the UN Food and Agriculture Organization expects crop yields to increase at about 1.4 percent per year through 2050. The upshot is that the food supply will increase faster than will the population, thereby increasing global food security.

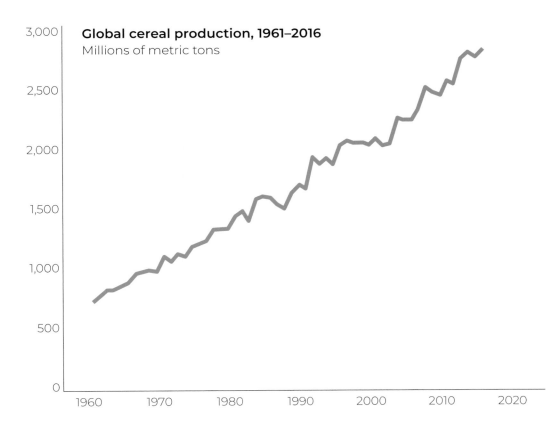

Global cereal production, 1961–2016
Millions of metric tons

Source: World Bank, "Cereal Production" chart.

YIELDS INCREASING

Farmers have always worked hard to boost their crop yields. Although estimates vary considerably, one historian concluded that farmers in the Roman Empire managed to coax from their fields an average across Italy of 540 kilograms (1,190 pounds) of wheat per hectare (2.5 acres) in the first century CE.[156] By the 16th century, farmers in England had nearly doubled annual yields to just over a metric ton of wheat per hectare. Average English wheat yields by 1800 rose 1.5 metric tons,[157] increasing to nearly 4 metric tons per hectare in 1965.[158] Corn yields in the United States averaged about 1.3 metric tons per hectare per year between 1866 and 1940. By 1960, yields rose to a bit more than 3.4 metric tons per hectare.[159] In the 18th and 19th centuries, farmers in southern China produced an average of just over 2 metric tons of rice per hectare.[160] In 1961, Chinese rice yields were still at 2 metric tons per hectare.[161] Grain yields began rising in the 20th century with hybridization, the synthesis of nitrogen fertilizer, improved pest and weed controls, and the development of genetically enhanced crops. Nobel Peace Prize laureate Norman Borlaug's crop-breeding breakthroughs ushered in the Green Revolution in the 1960s and 1970s.

> "Grain yields began rising in the 20th century with hybridization, the synthesis of nitrogen fertilizer, improved pest and weed controls, and the development of genetically enhanced crops. Nobel Peace Prize laureate Norman Borlaug's crop-breeding breakthroughs ushered in the Green Revolution in the 1960s and 1970s."

In 2018, British farmers harvested about 8 metric tons of wheat per hectare;[162] U.S. corn yields averaged 11 metric tons per hectare;[163] and Chinese rice yields were more than 7 metric tons per hectare.[164] That year also saw record-breaking individual farmer yields in British wheat at 16.79 metric tons and U.S. corn at 11 metric tons per hectare. A new Chinese hybrid "super rice" yields more than 18 metric tons per hectare.[165] As a result of ongoing progress, the World Bank reports that global cereal yields have increased from an average of 1.4 metric tons per hectare in 1961 to more than 4 metric tons per hectare in 2017.[166]

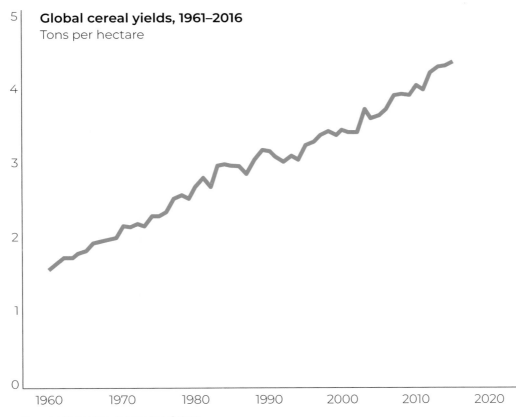

Global cereal yields, 1961–2016
Tons per hectare

Source: World Bank, "Cereal Yield" chart.

FARMING AND EATING MORE FISH

People around the world are eating more fish. The Food and Agriculture Organization (FAO) reports that, in 2016, humanity consumed 171 million metric tons of fish, including finfish, crustaceans, and mollusks. Overall, fish accounted for about 17 percent of animal protein and 7 percent of all proteins that were consumed by the world's population. According to the FAO, annual per capita fish consumption was around 6.5 kilograms (14 pounds) in 1950. Annual per capita consumption reached 20.3 kilograms (45 pounds) in 2016.

Wild-caught fish production rose between 1950 and 1996, from 18.71 million metric tons to 93.8 million metric tons.[167] The annual production in wild-capture fisheries has been essentially flat, hovering around 90 million metric tons over the past two decades.[168] Fish farming, however, has spectacularly boosted fish production.

In 1950, aquaculture produced less than a million metric tons of fish. In 2016, aquaculturists raised more than 80 million metric tons of fish—51 million metric tons on inland fish farms and 29 million metric tons at sea.[169] With regard to wild-caught fish, the percentage of stocks fished at biologically unsustainable levels has unfortunately increased from 10 percent

> "With regard to wild-caught fish, the percentage of stocks fished at biologically unsustainable levels has unfortunately increased from 10 percent in 1974 to 33.1 percent in 2015, with the largest increases in the late 1970s and 1980s. From the sustainability point of view, therefore, the growth of aquaculture is largely a welcome development."

in 1974 to 33.1 percent in 2015, with the largest increases in the late 1970s and 1980s. From the sustainability point of view, therefore, the growth of aquaculture is largely a welcome development.

The FAO projects that total world fish production (capture plus aquaculture) will expand to reach 201 million metric tons in 2030. The major growth in production is expected to originate from aquaculture, which is projected to reach 109 million metric tons in 2030. That amounts to 37 percent growth between 2016 and 2030.

Global fish consumption and production, 1950–2016
Million metric tons

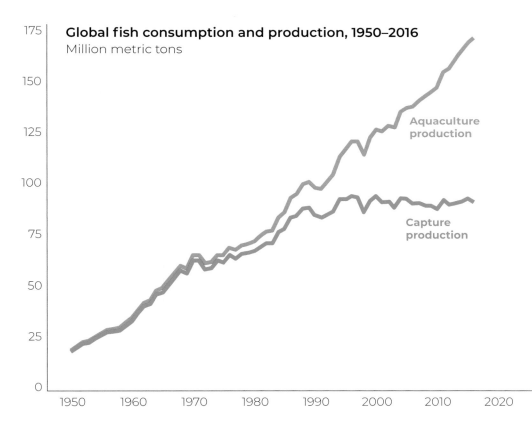

Aquaculture production

Capture production

Source: UN Food and Agriculture Organization, "World Review of Fisheries and Aquaculture," Part 1, Figure 1.

TREND 59
PROTEIN BOOM

People around the world are eating more meat and consuming more milk products. In 1941, Stanford University economist Merrill K. Bennett noted that as people become wealthier, they switch from simple starchy plant–dominated diets to those with more varied foods that include a range of vegetables, fruit, dairy products, and especially meat.

Currently, meat makes up 18 percent of global calories and 25 percent of global protein consumption. The Food and Agriculture Organization has documented the rising per capita consumption of meat and dairy products since the 1960s. The FAO reports that for the years 1964–1966, the global average consumption of meat—including beef, pork, sheep, goat, and poultry—was 24.4 kilograms

(54 pounds) per person per year. By 2015, that had increased to an annual average of 41.3 kilograms (91 pounds). The agency projects that average meat consumption will rise to 45.3 kilograms (100 pounds) per person per year by 2030.[170] Dairy consumption is increasing too. The FAO reports that for 1964–1966, per capita consumption of dairy products averaged 74 kilograms

> "In 1941, Stanford University economist Merrill K. Bennett noted that as people become wealthier, they switch from simple starchy plant–dominated diets to those with more varied foods that include a range of vegetables, fruit, dairy products, and especially meat."

(163 pounds) per year. That increased to 83 kilograms (183 pounds) by 2015 and is projected to rise to 90 kilograms (198 pounds) per person per year by 2030.

A 2017 FAO study also challenged some widely cited previous studies that claimed that it takes up to 20 kilograms (44 pounds) of grains to produce 1 kilogram (2.3 pounds) of beef. Contrary to those high estimates, the FAO researchers found that an average of only 3 kilograms (7 pounds) of cereals are needed to produce 1 kilogram of meat at the global level. The reason is 86 percent of the global livestock feed intake consists of fodder such as grasses and crop residues that are inedible by humans.[171]

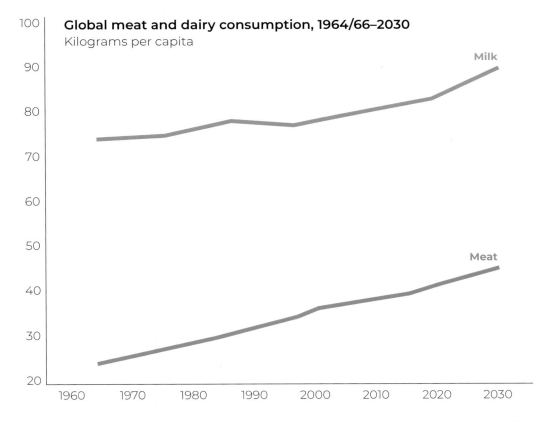

Global meat and dairy consumption, 1964/66–2030
Kilograms per capita

Milk

Meat

Source: Jelle Bruinsma, ed., *World Agriculture: Towards 2015/2030, An FAO Perspective* (Rome: FAO, 2003), pp. 86–87, tables 3.9 and 3.10.

FARM TRENDS

TECH TRENDS

TREND 60
ACCESS TO ELECTRICITY

"Access to electricity," the International Energy Agency notes, "is particularly crucial to human development as electricity is, in practice, indispensable for certain basic activities, such as lighting, refrigeration and the running of household appliances, and cannot easily be replaced by other forms of energy."[172] Today, practically everyone in advanced economies has access to electricity, and the process of electrification—which combines generation, building of the electric power grid, and supply of electricity to commercial and private entities—continues in developing countries.

Between 1990 and 2016, the proportion of the world's population with access to electricity rose from 71 percent to 87 percent. That's a 23 percent improvement. In South Asia, it rose from 41 percent to 86 percent. That amounts to an increase of 110 percent. In Latin America and the Caribbean, East Asia and the Pacific, and Middle East and North Africa regions, access to electricity increased from between 84 percent and 86 percent in 1990 to between 96 percent and 98 percent in 2016. Sub-Saharan Africa saw the greatest growth in access to electricity.

> "Today, practically everyone in advanced economies has access to electricity, and the process of electrification—which combines generation, building of the electric power grid, and supply of electricity to commercial and private entities—continues in developing countries."

The rise from 16 percent to 43 percent represents an astonishing improvement of 169 percent.[173]

As the International Energy Agency notes in its report Energy Access Outlook 2017: "The number of people without access to electricity fell to 1.1 billion in 2016 from 1.7 billion in 2000. It is on track to decline to 674 million by 2030. Since 2012, more than 100 million people per year have gained electricity access, an acceleration from the rate of 62 million people per year seen between 2000 and 2012."[174] In the meantime, the process of electrification in Sub-Saharan Africa has outpaced that region's rapid population growth in 2014. That means that the number of Africans without access to electricity has finally started to decline.

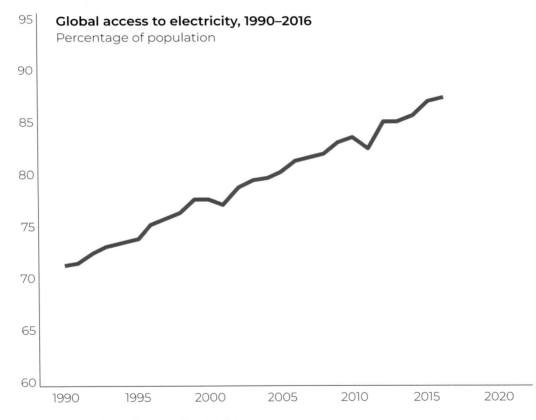

Global access to electricity, 1990–2016
Percentage of population

Source: World Bank, "Access to Electricity" chart.

LIGHTING COSTS NEAR NOTHING NOW

To light the night, our ancestors initially used wood, later burning vegetable fats, such as sesame oil. Next came candles made from beeswax, spermaceti derived from sperm whales, and tallow rendered from animal fat. Later lamps were fueled by coal gas and kerosene. Electric lighting emerged at the end of the 19th century, first as a luxury and now as a basic component of modern life in most countries.

Both the efficiency and the cost of lighting have changed a great deal. In 1996, William D. Nordhaus of Yale University calculated that open fire produced a mere 0.00235 lumens per watt. (A lumen is a measure of how much visible light is emitted by a source. Lumens per watt refers to the energy efficiency of lighting. A traditional 60-watt incandescent bulb in the United States, for example, produces 860 lumens.) A sesame-oil lamp could produce 0.0597 lumens per watt; a spermaceti candle, 0.1009 lumens; whale oil, 0.1346 lumens; and an early town gas lamp, 0.2464 lumens.[175] In 1883, an electric filament bulb emitted a then-astonishing 2.6 lumens per watt, rising eventually to 14.1667 lumens by 1990. In 1992, compact fluorescent light bulbs greatly exceeded incandescent bulbs'

> **"Nordhaus estimates that our Paleolithic ancestors labored 58 hours, mostly gathering wood, to 'buy' 1,000 lumen-hours of light."**

efficiency by delivering 68.2778 lumens per watt.

Those amazing efficiency improvements collapsed the price of lighting. Nordhaus estimates that our Paleolithic ancestors labored 58 hours, mostly gathering wood, to "buy" 1,000 lumen-hours of light. (A lumen-hour is a unit of luminous energy, equal to that emitted in 1 hour by a light source emitting a luminous flux of 1 lumen.) By 1800, it took about 5.4 hours, and by 1900, it took 0.22 hours. In 1992, 1,000 lumen-hours required 0.00012 hours of human labor. That amounts to a reduction of close to 100 percent.

Global hours worked to produce light, 1800–1992
Hours per 1,000 lumen-hours

Source: William D. Nordhaus, "Do Real-Output and Real-Wage Measures Capture Reality? The History of Lighting Suggests Not," in *The Economics of New Goods*, eds. Timothy F. Bresnahan and Robert J. Gordon (Chicago: University of Chicago Press, 1996), p. 36.

SOLAR POWER EVER CHEAPER

The prices of silicon solar photovoltaic cells will continue their steep exponential decline, according to the *New Energy Outlook* 2018 report from Bloomberg's New Energy Finance (BNEF) group. According to the BNEF, the average price of silicon photovoltaic (PV) cells fell from $76 per watt in 1977 to $4 per watt in 2008, a drop of nearly 95 percent. Since 2008, the price of PVs has fallen to $0.24 per watt, another drop of nearly 95 percent.[176] That downward trajectory tracks technological improvements in the efficiency of solar cells, as well as increasing economies of scale. With regard to the latter, solar cell prices seem to be following Swanson's law, named for Richard Swanson, the founder of U.S. solar-cell manufacturer SunPower. Swanson suggests that the cost of PV cells falls by 20 percent with each doubling of global manufacturing capacity. The pattern is a product of constantly improving manufacturing processes: more automation, better quality control, materials reduction, and so forth. As of 2018, BNEF reports that global wind and solar developers had installed their first trillion watts of power-generation capacity, and it projects that the next trillion watts in renewable generation will be completed within the next five years. In 2016, total world electric power-generation capacity stood at 6.2 trillion watts.

As the result of ever-falling costs, the Bloomberg analysts project that by 2050, wind and solar technologies will generate almost 50 percent of total electricity globally, with hydropower, nuclear power, and other renewables pushing total zero-carbon electricity up to 71 percent. The big loser will be coal, with its share of global electricity generation shrinking from 38 percent today to 11 percent in 2050. And silicon solar cells may be superseded by even cheaper and more-efficient sun-harvesting technologies, such as perovskite cells at a projected $0.10 per watt.

> "As the result of ever-falling costs, the Bloomberg analysts project that by 2050, wind and solar technologies will generate almost 50 percent of total electricity globally, with hydropower, nuclear power, and other renewables pushing total zero-carbon electricity up to 71 percent."

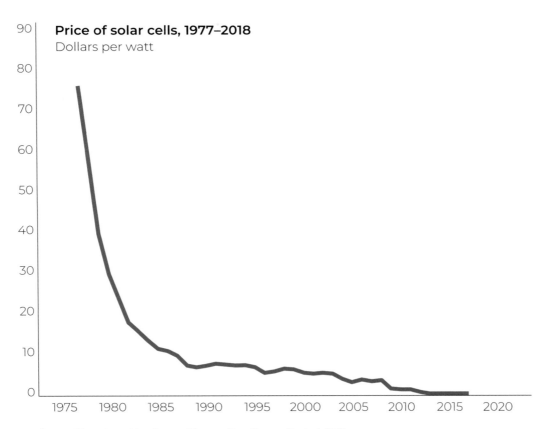

Price of solar cells, 1977–2018
Dollars per watt

90

80

70

60

50

40

30

20

10

0

1975   1980   1985   1990   1995   2000   2005   2010   2015   2020

Source: Bloomberg New Energy Finance, *New Energy Outlook 2015*.

CLEAN DRINKING WATER

Before the 19th century, people didn't know about the germ theory of disease. Consequently, most people paid little attention to the water they drank. The results were often catastrophic, since contaminated water spreads infectious diseases, including dysentery, typhoid, polio, and cholera. Consider the 1854 cholera outbreak in London. The city lacked adequate sanitation infrastructure. Cowsheds and slaughterhouses lined the city's streets. Animal droppings and discarded carcasses added to human waste that often overwhelmed primitive sewers beneath the city's streets.

London was then supplied with drinking water by two water companies. The first drew its water from the Thames upstream of the city. The second drew its water from the Thames downstream of the city. After cholera broke out, John Snow, an English physician, found higher concentrations of the disease in those parts of London that were supplied by the second water company. He hypothesized that cholera spread via contaminated water. Snow's discovery inspired the construction of improved sanitation facilities in industrializing countries of the 19th century and continues to influence public health initiatives in the developing world today. That's clearly necessary. According to the World Health Organization's estimates, 361,000 children under the age of five died in 2015 because of inadequate sanitation and lack of access to clean water.[177] Much progress is, nevertheless, being made. Between 1990 and 2015, access to improved water sources rose from 76 percent of the world's population to 91 percent. That amounts to 2.6 billion people, or over a third of the world's population.[178] Put differently, 285,000 people have gained access to clean water each day over that period. Consequently, the number of people without access to clean water has fallen from 1.26 billion to 666 million.[179]

> **"According to the World Health Organization's estimates, 361,000 children under the age of five died in 2015 because of inadequate sanitation and lack of access to clean water."**

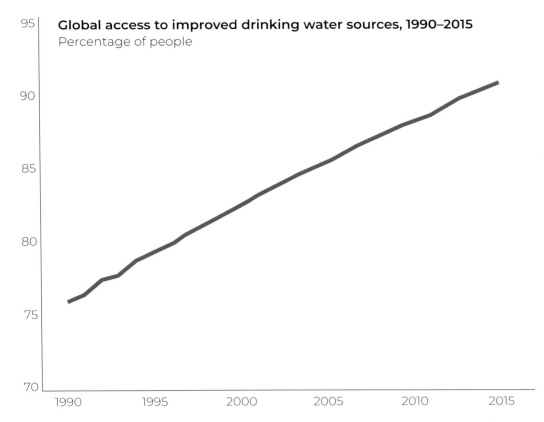

Global access to improved drinking water sources, 1990–2015
Percentage of people

95	
90	
85	
80	
75	
70	

1990   1995   2000   2005   2010   2015

Source: United Nations Statistics Division, Department of Economic and Social Affairs, "Millennium Development Goals Indicators."

IMPROVING SANITATION

The vital need for a hygienic separation of human and animal bodily wastes from human contact may seem obvious to most people today, but for millennia that was not the case. Before the discovery of the germ theory of disease, and the subsequent public health campaigns and construction of an adequate sanitation infrastructure in most of the world, people and waste commingled with catastrophic results. Countless millions of people got sick or died after they unknowingly ingested waste infected with pathogens causing such diseases as cholera, hepatitis, trachoma, polio, and others.

Some cultures paid better attention to cleanliness than others. Ancient Rome, for example, built numerous public baths and a sophisticated system of sewers, which enabled the city to sustain a population of more than 1 million people—a feat that would not be replicated in Europe until the 19th century, in London and Paris. In the rural areas, people lived with their animals, including chickens and cows, and used both animal and human waste to fertilize their crops— an extremely dangerous practice compounded by the fact that people could go throughout much of their lives without ever washing their hands.

Today, poor sanitation is mostly limited to very poor countries. In Sub-Saharan Africa, for example, a mere 30 percent

> "Some cultures paid better attention to cleanliness than others. Ancient Rome, for example, built numerous public baths and a sophisticated system of sewers, which enabled the city to sustain a population of more than 1 million people—a feat that would not be replicated in Europe until the 19th century, in London and Paris."

of the population had access to an improved sanitation facility (i.e., one that hygienically separates human excreta from human contact) in 2015. That was an improvement on 1990, when only 24 percent did so. In other parts of the world, progress was much faster. In South Asia, which includes populous countries like India and Bangladesh, the share of the population with access to improved sanitation rose from 20 percent to 45 percent over the same period. Globally, it increased from 53 percent to 68 percent.[180] The United Nations' aim of ending open defecation by 2030 is probably too optimistic for regions like Sub-Saharan Africa and South Asia, but East Asia, Latin America, and the Middle East should be able to reach the European level of improved sanitation facilities (93 percent) by 2030.

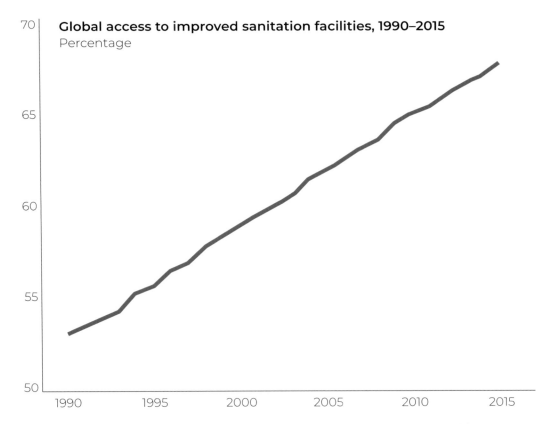

Global access to improved sanitation facilities, 1990–2015
Percentage

70

65

60

55

50

1990   1995   2000   2005   2010   2015

Source: United Nations, "Target 7.C: Halve, by 2015, the Proportion of People without Sustainable Access to Safe Drinking Water and Basic Sanitation," Millennium Development Goals.

TREND 65
MOBILE PHONE REVOLUTION

In the 1987 Oliver Stone movie *Wall Street*, Gordon Gekko, an immensely wealthy investor played by actor Michael Douglas, walks on a beach, watching the sunrise and talking on his Motorola DynaTac 8000X cellphone. When it was released in 1983, DynaTac was the world's first handheld mobile phone. It weighed two pounds, took 10 hours to charge and offered 30 minutes of talk time. In 1984, the phone cost $3,995.[181] That's $10,277 in 2018 dollars. As late as 1990, cellphones were so expensive that only 2 percent of Americans owned them.[182] Today, cellphones in the United States outnumber people.

Over time, cellphones became more powerful and useful. They also became smaller and cheaper. In 2016, 73 percent of the population of Sub-Saharan Africa, the world's poorest region, owned what was once a plaything of the superrich.[183]

A Nigerian coal miner in South Africa can use a phone app to send money to his mother in Lagos. A Congolese fisherman can be warned about approaching inclement weather. A Masai herdsman can find out the price of milk in Nairobi.

By adopting cellular technology, poor countries were able to leapfrog an important bottleneck in their economic development, the landline phone. Globally, fixed phone line coverage peaked at 21.4 percent in 2002. In

"From the Arab Spring in 2010 to the pro-democracy protests in Hong Kong in 2014, cellphones, smartphones, and a variety of social media apps enabled ordinary people to access censored content and to share it."

Sub-Saharan Africa, fixed phone line coverage never reached more than 1.57 percent of the population. Today, all of humanity's knowledge can be accessed via cellphone easily and instantaneously.

Finally, consider the impact of cellular technology on politics. From the Arab Spring in 2010 to the pro-democracy protests in Hong Kong in 2014, cellphones, smartphones, and a variety of social media apps enabled ordinary people to access censored content and to share it. Cellular technology enables the citizenry in authoritarian countries to communicate in encrypted ways and to organize.

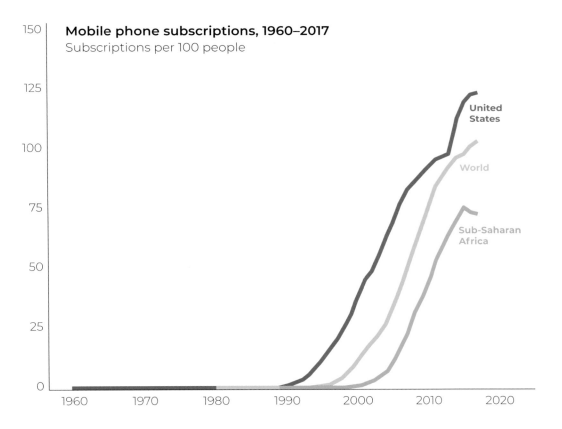

Mobile phone subscriptions, 1960–2017
Subscriptions per 100 people

United States

World

Sub-Saharan Africa

Source: World Bank, *World Development Indicators*. "Mobile Cellular Subscriptions (per 100 People)" chart.

INTERNET EXPLOSION

The internet is one of the greatest inventions of all time. First, it is a repository of human knowledge. Search engines provide answers to virtually all questions. New books are easily accessible in digital and audio forms, while old books have been digitized en masse. Publishing and broadcasting have been democratized. People can share their ideas easily and, if need be, anonymously. Second, the internet enables easy communication. International phone calls were once very expensive. Today, video chats allow face-to-face conversations with anyone, anywhere.

Third, the internet is a productivity enhancer. Online banking allows people to conveniently view their balances, pay their bills, and make other transactions. Online shopping allows buyers to access most goods and services, compare their prices, and read product reviews. Sellers can reach more people than could ever fit in a retail store. The internet also makes it easier to raise, remit, and donate money. It allows employees to work from home, thus avoiding costly and time-consuming commutes. Online hiring gives employers access to a worldwide talent pool. Finally, the internet has become one of the main sources of popular entertainment, allowing people to access movies, shows, concerts, and live events from the comfort of their living rooms. Thankfully, internet use is rapidly growing. Between 1990 and

"Mark Zuckerberg's Facebook and Elon Musk's SpaceX are working on a system of internet satellites designed to provide low-cost internet service from Earth's orbit. Google, in the meantime, wants to launch high-altitude internet balloons to the stratosphere, where they will catch a ride on wind currents to their destinations in the developing world."

2016, the share of the world's population with access to the internet rose from zero to 46 percent. It is expected to rise to 52 percent by 2020. In 2016, the highest number of internet users was in North America (78 percent) and the lowest was in Sub-Saharan Africa (20 percent).[184] Those numbers are likely to increase, because the cost of the internet "transit price"—or sending data from one computer to another—fell from $1,200 per megabit per second in 1998 to $0.63 in 2015.[185]

Plans are also afoot to bring the internet to some of the poorest people in the world. Currently, internet traffic flows through expensive fiber-optic cables. Mark Zuckerberg's Facebook and Elon Musk's SpaceX are working on a system of internet satellites designed to provide low-cost internet service from Earth's orbit. Google, in the meantime, wants to launch high-altitude internet balloons to the stratosphere, where they will catch a ride on wind currents to their destinations in the developing world.

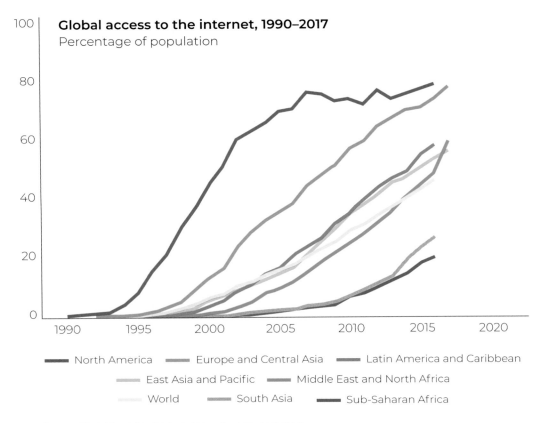

Global access to the internet, 1990–2017
Percentage of population

Legend:
- North America
- Europe and Central Asia
- Latin America and Caribbean
- East Asia and Pacific
- Middle East and North Africa
- World
- South Asia
- Sub-Saharan Africa

Source: World Bank, "Individuals Using the Internet" chart.

VASTLY CHEAPER COMPUTATION

In 1980, Seagate Technology introduced its ST506 5.25-inch 5-megabyte hard drive[186] at a cost of $1,500 per unit, or $4,860 in 2018 dollars.[187] Roughly calculated, that means that a gigabyte (1,000 megabytes) of storage would have cost $300,000, or just shy of $1 million in 2018 dollars. Generally speaking, a gigabyte can store information that is the equivalent to about 3,000 books or 500 photographs.

In late 2018, one could purchase a Seagate BarraCuda ST6000DM003

> **"Cheaper memory is also a crucial factor in today's era of nearly free computing. In 2017, the International Data Corporation projected that by 2025, humanity's global datasphere will be generating 175 zettabytes (175 trillion gigabytes) of data annually, a tenfold increase from the amount of information created in 2016."**

8-terabyte hard drive for $199.27. That means that the cost of storing data had fallen to $0.019 per gigabyte. In real dollars, that's a decline of more than 99.99 percent.[188]

The measure of computational power is also steadily increasing. The speed of computer processors can be expressed in flops (floating-point operations per second). One billion flops is called a gigaflop.

As late as 1984, the cost of 1 gigaflop was $18.7 million ($46.4 million in 2018 dollars). By 2000, the price per gigaflop had fallen to $640 ($956 in 2018 dollars). In late 2017, the cost had dropped to $0.03 per gigaflop. That is a decline of more than 99.99 percent in real dollars since 2000.

Ever-cheaper memory is one the chief enabling technologies that has made cheap computation possible. Consider that in 1981, IBM introduced the Model 5150 personal computer containing 40 kilobytes of read-only memory and

16 kilobytes of user memory. The whole setup—including computer, keyboard, and monochrome monitor—weighed 51 pounds. Its price was $1,565 ($4,535 in 2018 dollars).[189]

In late 2018, a not especially fancy Best Buy Insignia tablet and keyboard combo weighing less than 2 pounds was selling for $120. The Insignia comes preloaded with Windows 10, Wi-Fi, and 32 gigabytes of memory. Ignoring the vast improvement in functionality and convenience, that's a price reduction of more than 97 percent.

Cheaper memory is also a crucial factor in today's era of nearly free computing. In 2017, the International Data Corporation projected that by 2025, humanity's global datasphere will be generating 175 zettabytes (175 trillion gigabytes) of data annually, a tenfold increase from the amount of information created in 2016.[190]

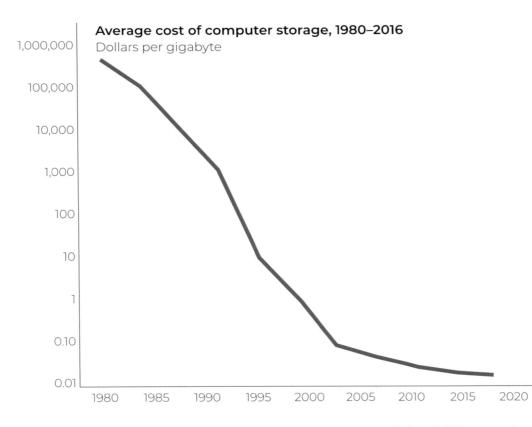

Average cost of computer storage, 1980–2016
Dollars per gigabyte

Source: AcceleratingBiz, "Average Magnetic Storage Price Fell Drastically from $437,500 per Gigabyte in 1980 to $0.019 in 2016, a 99.99% Decline," Proof Point, October 5, 2017.

GLOBAL TOURISM RISES (PRE-PANDEMIC)

As with so much else in the past, traveling was difficult and often dangerous. Roads were rutted, sailing hazardous, and highwaymen and pirates numerous. Most private travel was undertaken for trade or pilgrimages. Travel for pleasure or out of curiosity is a relatively modern phenomenon. It was popularized, at least in the European context, by wealthy young noblemen who, beginning in the 17th century, started to undertake the "grand tour" of European cities, including Paris, Venice, Florence, and Rome, to take in the ancient monuments and works of art. These educational rites of passage were expensive and time-consuming. Consequently, they were restricted to the rich "gentlemen of leisure." The cost and convenience of travel dramatically improved with the advent of the steam engine. In the 19th century, trains enabled unprecedented numbers of people to travel within countries, while steamships sped up international travel. Early steamships cut the sailing time from London to New York from about six weeks to about 15 days. By the middle of the 20th century, ocean liners like the *SS United States* could make the trip in fewer than four days. Today, an airplane can fly between the two cities in eight hours.

According to the World Tourism Organization, 524 million people got to travel to a foreign country in 1995. That number grew to 1.34 billion in 2017. That's a 156 percent increase.

Over the same period, the share of global travel undertaken by residents of high-income countries declined from 72 percent to 61 percent. The share of travelers from upper-middle-income countries, such as Botswana and Mexico, rose from 8.5 percent to 26 percent. Residents of lower-middle-income countries, such as Nigeria and Pakistan, increased their share of global travel from 2.5 percent to 10 percent.[191] A luxury that was once reserved for a tiny sliver of society is now available to an ever-increasing number of people throughout the world.

> "The cost and convenience of travel dramatically improved with the advent of the steam engine. In the 19th century, trains enabled unprecedented numbers of people to travel within countries, while steamships sped up international travel."

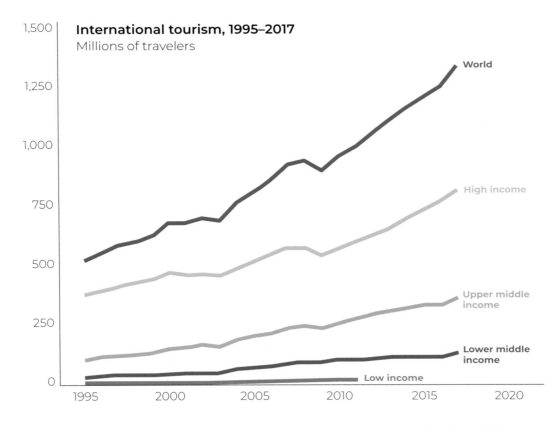

International tourism, 1995–2017
Millions of travelers

- World
- High income
- Upper middle income
- Lower middle income
- Low income

1,500

1,250

1,000

750

500

250

0

1995   2000   2005   2010   2015   2020

Source: World Bank, *World Development Indicators*, "International Tourism, Number of Arrivals" chart.

TARIFFS ARE FALLING

"On the social front, there is overwhelming evidence that trade openness is a more trustworthy friend of the poor than protectionism. Few countries have grown rapidly without a simultaneous rapid expansion of trade. In turn, rapid growth has almost always led to reduction in poverty," writes Columbia University economist Arvind Panagariya.[192] However, freedom of trade has always been impeded by "protectionism," the economic policy of restricting imports from other countries. Historically speaking, taxes on imports have been the favorite tool of the protectionists. With regard to these "tariffs," the world has made a lot of progress.

> **"Historically speaking, taxes on imports have been the favorite tool of the protectionists. With regard to these 'tariffs,' the world has made a lot of progress."**

"Applied tariffs" are the taxes that countries actually apply on imports. They are not to be confused with "bound tariffs," which denote the maximum taxes on imports countries can impose under international trade conventions. As such, applied tariffs tend to be lower than bound tariffs. Singapore, for example, can levy a 9.6 percent tariff on imports from overseas (i.e., a bound tariff). In reality, Singaporean import duties amount to only 0.2 percent (i.e., applied tariff).

Between 1988 and 2017, the applied weighted mean tariff rate on all products declined from 4.8 percent to 2.6 percent. That's a decline of 46 percent. South Asia, the world's most protectionist region, reduced its tariffs from 88 percent in 1989 to 6 percent in 2017. Tariffs in Latin America and the Caribbean fell from 32 percent to 3.5 percent. They fell from 16 percent to 5.7 percent in Sub-Saharan Africa.[193] In spite of a recent bout of protectionism in the United States, American tariffs amounted to only 1.66 percent in 2017. Thus, Europe, North America, and East Asia continue to be the leaders in tariff reduction, though no region is fully exempt from implementing nontariff restrictions on trade, including import licenses, production standards, phytosanitary requirements, administrative and bureaucratic delays, and foreign exchange controls.

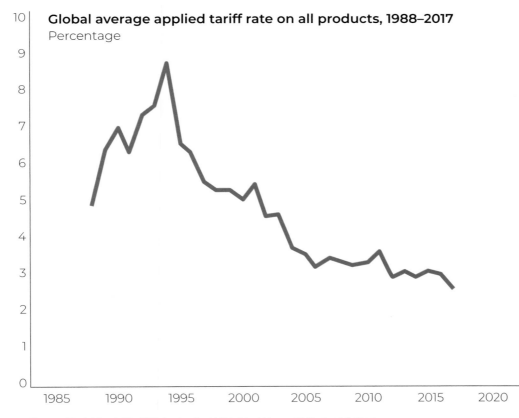

Global average applied tariff rate on all products, 1988–2017
Percentage

U.S. TRENDS

SHARE OF SPENDING ON HOUSEHOLD BASICS DECLINES

As American households grew wealthier during the 20th century, they spent an ever-smaller proportion of their incomes on the basic necessities of food, clothing, and housing. In 1900, the average U.S. family spent $769 per year (in 1900 dollars), and nearly 80 percent of that went to pay for food (42.5 percent), clothing (14 percent), and housing (23.3 percent), according to the U.S. Bureau of Labor Statistics. Only 19 percent of U.S. families owned a home, while 81 percent were renters. The average new home was approximately 700 square feet, providing about 140 square feet per person in a family.[194] By 1972, household expenses averaged $8,348 per year (in 1972 dollars), and the percentage devoted to basic necessities had dropped to 57.9 percent, of which 19.3 percent was for food, 7.8 percent for clothing, and 30.8 percent for housing. Most Americans, 58.8 percent, owned their homes, while 36.8 percent were renters. The average size of a new home was about 1,700 square feet, providing about 570 square feet per household member.[195]

According to the latest figures from the Bureau of Labor Statistics, the average American household spent $60,060 in 2017. By the second decade of the 21st century, American household expenditures on basic necessities had fallen to below 50 percent, from 80 percent in 1900. In 2018, household outlays on food were at 12.9 percent (of which more than 36 percent was spent on food consumption away from the home, such as in restaurants), clothing at 3 percent, and housing at 32.8 percent.[196] In 2018, the homeownership rate was 63.7 percent, and the size of new single-family homes averaged 2,641 square feet, affording each family member an area of 1,016 square feet.[197]

> "In 2017, the homeownership rate was 63.7 percent, and the size of new single-family homes averaged 2,616 square feet, affording each family member an area of 1,006 square feet."

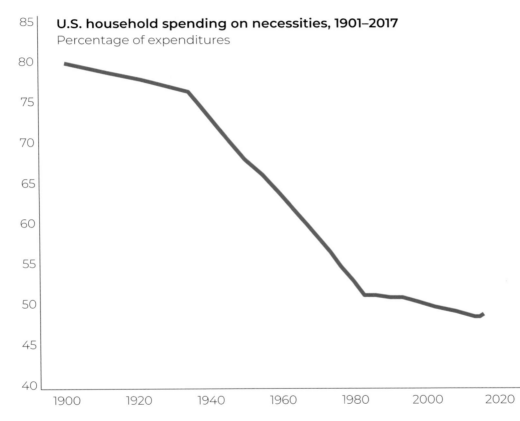

U.S. household spending on necessities, 1901–2017
Percentage of expenditures

Sources: For 1901–2003 data, Elaine L. Chao and Kathleen P. Utgoff, "100 Years of U.S. Consumer Spending: Data for the Nation, New York City, and Boston," U.S. Department of Labor Report 991, August 3, 2006; and for 2016–2017 data, see U.S. Bureau of Labor Statistics, "Consumer Expenditures–2018," Economic News Release, September 10, 2019.

COST AND ADOPTION OF NEW TECHNOLOGIES

Economic prosperity is often measured using personal income or wealth. Neither of those two measures, however, provides a full picture of people's material well-being. Standards of living can increase because of both falling prices and rising incomes. Even people with falling incomes can be better-off, as long as the cost of living decreases at a faster pace than incomes shrink.

Consider the cost and adoption of home appliances. In 1968, for example, a 23-inch Admiral color TV cost $2,544 in 2018 U.S. dollars, or 120 hours of labor in the manufacturing sector.[198] In

> **"It took about a half century from the invention of the telephone to the time when 50 percent of U.S. households owned one. In contrast, after only 12 years of smartphones hitting the stores, 50 percent of individual Americans possessed one."**

2018, a 24-inch Sceptre high-definition LED TV cost $99.99, or 4.7 hours of labor at the average hourly wage in the manufacturing sector.[199] That's a reduction of 96 percent in human effort. In 1968, a 16.2-cubic-foot refrigerator cost $2,725 (in 2018 U.S. dollars), or 128 hours of labor.[200] In 2018, an 18-cubic-foot refrigerator cost $497, or 23 hours of labor.[201] That's a reduction of 97 percent in human labor.

Over the same period, the cost of a 5,000-Btu air conditioner fell from $640, or 30 hours of work, to $136, or 6.4 hours of work—an 80 percent decline (both prices are in 2018 U.S. dollars).[202]

When Texas Instruments introduced the TI-2500 Datamath handheld calculator in 1972, it cost $905 (in 2018 dollars) or 43 hours of labor.[203] The company's solar-powered TI30X IIS scientific calculator sold for $8.88 in 2018, or about 25 minutes of work.[204] That's a decline of 99 percent. In 1981, the cheapest IBM personal computer cost $4,459 (in 2018 U.S. dollars), or 210

hours of labor.[205] An Insignia tablet and keyboard combo cost $120 in 2018, or 5.6 hours of labor.[206] Ignoring the vast increase in functionality, that's a reduction of 97 percent. As late as 1971, only 43.3 percent of all U.S. households had a color television. By 2005, 97.4 percent of poor U.S. households owned a color TV.[207] Similar stories can be told of washing machines, dishwashers, clothes dryers, refrigerators, freezers, stoves, and vacuum cleaners. And the speed of adoption of new products is increasing. It took about a half century from the invention of the telephone to the time when 50 percent of U.S. households owned one. In contrast, after only 12 years of smartphones hitting the stores, 50 percent of individual Americans possessed one.

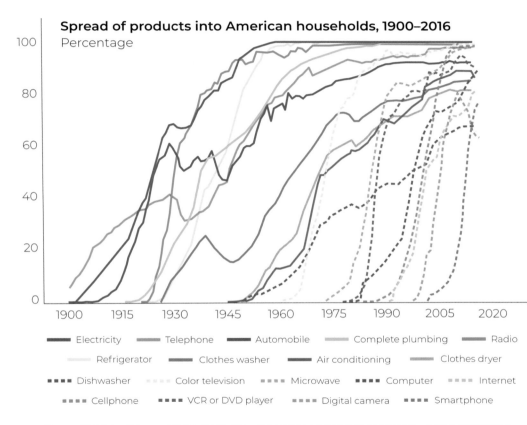

Spread of products into American households, 1900–2016
Percentage

Legend:
- Electricity
- Telephone
- Automobile
- Complete plumbing
- Radio
- Refrigerator
- Clothes washer
- Air conditioning
- Clothes dryer
- Dishwasher
- Color television
- Microwave
- Computer
- Internet
- Cellphone
- VCR or DVD player
- Digital camera
- Smartphone

Source: W. Michael Cox and Richard Alm, "Onward and Upward! Bet on Capitalism—It Works," William J. O'Neil Center for Global Markets and Freedom 2015–2016 Annual Report.

VIOLENT CRIME RATES ARE FALLING STEEPLY

A March 2019 Gallup poll reported that 47 percent and 28 percent of Americans, respectively, worried about crime and violence a great deal or a fair amount.[208] In fact, polls found persistently high levels of concern over crime during the past decade, even though violent crime rates have been falling steeply for the past two decades.

The murder rate in the United States rose sharply from about 5 per 100,000 residents in the 1960s to eventually hover at around 9 murders per 100,000 people in the 1970s, where that rate remained for two decades. It started to fall after 1995.[209] In 2017, the FBI reported that the homicide rate was 5.3 per 100,000 residents.[210] The murder rate is now basically back down to the levels experienced in the 1960s.

The violent crime rate—including rape, robbery, and aggravated assault—also escalated rapidly after the 1960s, eventually peaking at 758.2 per 100,000 residents in 1991.[211] In 2018, the violent crime rate was down to 368.9 per 100,000 persons, slightly higher than the rate experienced in 1970. That's a reduction of about 50 percent.

In Gallup's 2017 poll, nearly half of respondents said that they believed that immigrants make the crime situation worse. In fact, most studies find that immigrants, both legal and undocumented, commit crimes at a lower rate than do native-born citizens. For example, a 2018 study in the journal *Criminology*—which examined immigration and crime data from all 50 states between 1990 and 2014—found: "Undocumented immigration does not increase violence. Rather, the relationship between undocumented immigration and violent crime is generally negative."[212]

> "In Gallup's 2017 poll, nearly half of respondents said that they believed that immigrants make the crime situation worse. In fact, most studies find that immigrants, both legal and undocumented, commit crimes at a lower rate than do native-born citizens."

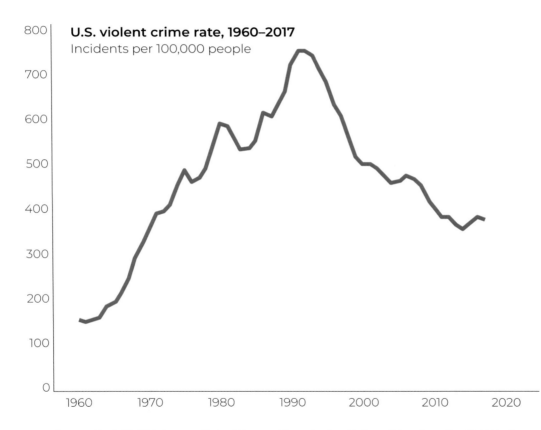

U.S. violent crime rate, 1960–2017
Incidents per 100,000 people

Sources: For 1960–2014 data, see Federal Bureau of Investigation, Uniform Crime Reporting Statistics (online), "State-by-State and National Crime Estimates by Year(s)"; and for 2015–2017 data, see FBI, UCR, "Crime in the United States, 2018," Table 1.

DECLINING RACIST ATTITUDES

Back in 1958, only 4 percent of whites were in favor of intermarriage between blacks and whites, according to historical data from the Gallup Organization. In 1963, only 38 percent of whites opposed laws against intermarriage.[213] By 2002, when the question was last asked, 90 percent of whites opposed laws against intermarriage. Black opposition to laws against intermarriage increased from 82 percent in 1980 to 96 percent

"Despite extensive changes in racial attitudes and considerable civil rights progress, a 2019 Gallup poll update reported that 54 percent of U.S. whites think that black-white relations are generally good, whereas only 40 percent of blacks do. Although progress has been substantial, work clearly remains to be done."

in 2002. In 1972, 76 percent of blacks approved of interracial marriage. By 2013, approval of interracial marriage had increased to 87 percent among white Americans.

According to 2016 Gallup poll data, 69 percent of African Americans think that the civil rights situation for black citizens has greatly or somewhat improved over the course of their lifetimes. The corresponding figure is 77 percent for white Americans.

In a 2016 study on historical U.S. trends in racial attitudes, researchers at the University of Illinois report that white approval of school racial integration rose from just 32 percent in 1942 to 96 percent by 1995.[214] Since polling of their community began in 1972, black support for school integration has been universal.

In 1944, only 45 percent of whites agreed that blacks should have "as good a chance as white people to get

any kind of job." That opinion rose to 97 percent of whites by 1972. In 1958, only 37 percent of whites said they would vote for a black candidate for president. By 1997, that figure had risen to 95 percent.

The University of Illinois researchers note, "One of the most substantial changes in white racial attitudes has been the movement from very substantial opposition to the principle of racial equality to one of almost universal support."[215]

Despite extensive changes in racial attitudes and considerable civil rights progress, a 2019 Gallup poll update reported that 54 percent of U.S. whites think that black-white relations are generally good, whereas only 40 percent of blacks do. Although progress has been substantial, work clearly remains to be done.

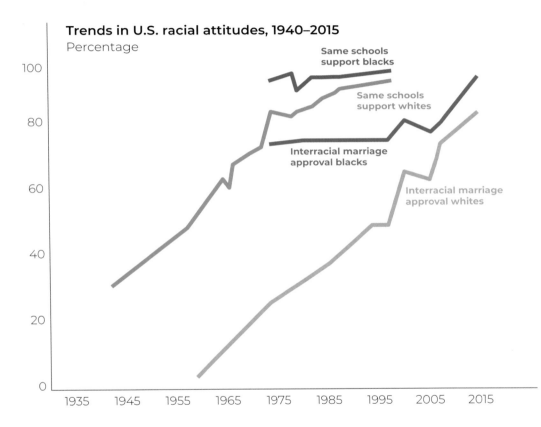

Trends in U.S. racial attitudes, 1940–2015

Percentage

- Same schools support blacks
- Same schools support whites
- Interracial marriage approval blacks
- Interracial marriage approval whites

100

80

60

40

20

0

1935　1945　1955　1965　1975　1985　1995　2005　2015

Source: Maria Krysan and Sarah Patton Moberg, "Trends in Racial Attitudes," August 25, 2016, University of Illinois Institute of Government and Public Affairs.

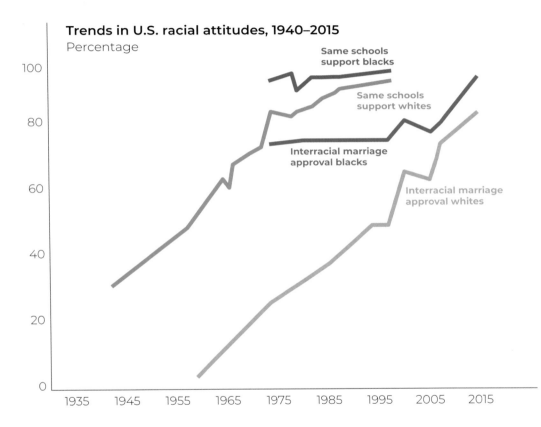

AIR POLLUTION IS FALLING STEEPLY

The Clean Air Act of 1970 requires the Environmental Protection Agency to set National Ambient Air Quality Standards for six common air pollutants: carbon monoxide, lead, nitrogen dioxide, ozone, particulates such as smoke, and sulfur dioxide.

That doesn't mean that Americans didn't care about the air they breathed before 1970. Many American cities responded to rising noxious levels of air pollution by adopting smoke abatement ordinances in the late 19th century. As a result of local municipal action, emissions of smoke, soot, ozone, and sulfur dioxide had been falling for decades before the creation of the EPA. For example, ambient sulfur dioxide had fallen by 58 percent in New York City during the seven years preceding the adoption of the Clean Air Act.[216] Between 1980 and 2018, according to the EPA, emissions of carbon monoxide fell by 73 percent; lead, by 99 percent; nitrogen oxides, by 62 percent; compounds from automobile exhaust associated with ozone, by 55 percent; sulfur dioxide, by 90 percent; and particulates, by 61 percent.[217] The EPA reports that between 1970 and 2018, U.S. gross domestic product increased 275 percent, vehicle miles traveled increased 191 percent, energy consumption increased 49 percent, and the U.S. population grew by 60 percent. In addition, carbon dioxide emissions increased by 22 percent. During the same period, total emission of the six principal air pollutants dropped by 74 percent.[218]

More than two decades ago, economics scholars devised the environmental Kuznets curve hypothesis that posits that environmental conditions initially deteriorate as economic growth takes off, but later improve when citizens with rising incomes demand better-quality environmental amenities. Considerable evidence now backs the notion that increasing wealth from economic growth correlates with a cleaner natural environment—that is to say, richer becomes cleaner.

> "Many American cities responded to rising noxious levels of air pollution by adopting smoke abatement ordinances in the late 19th century. As a result of local municipal action, emissions of smoke, soot, ozone, and sulfur dioxide had been falling for decades before the creation of the EPA."

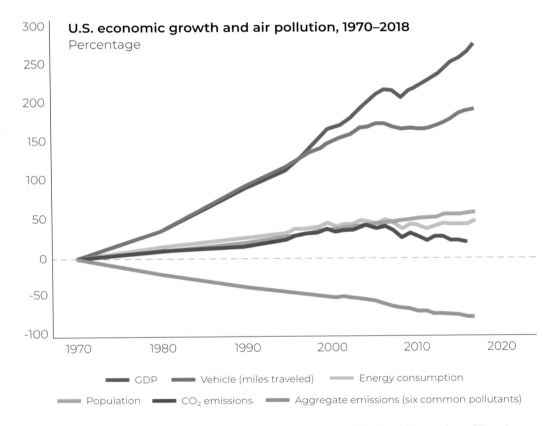

U.S. economic growth and air pollution, 1970–2018
Percentage

Legend:
- GDP
- Vehicle (miles traveled)
- Energy consumption
- Population
- CO_2 emissions
- Aggregate emissions (six common pollutants)

Source: U.S. Environmental Protection Agency, *Our Nation's Air 2018* (website) "Comparison of Growth Areas and Emissions, 1970–2018."
Note: GDP = gross domestic product

TREND 75
BIGGER AND BETTER HOUSING

The size of personal living space is an important indicator of human well-being. The primitive dwellings of our farming ancestors, which they built for themselves, were generally overcrowded and unhygienic. Until relatively recently, for example, it was not uncommon for two or three generations of the same family to live under the same roof, often sleeping together in the only heated room in the house. Humans often shared their living space with their livestock to keep the latter safe from predators and thieves. That created a fertile ground for vermin and parasites, leading to periodic outbreaks of deadly diseases.

> "Until relatively recently, for example, it was not uncommon for two or three generations of the same family to live under the same roof, often sleeping together in the only heated room in the house."

As late as 1900, a regular American home contained between 700 and 1,200 square feet of living space. According to the National Association of Home Builders, "More than 20 percent of the U.S. population lived in crowded units, with entire families often sharing one or two rooms." To make matters worse, only 50 percent of U.S. homes contained a bathroom. Half of the population, in other words, had to use communal bathrooms or an outhouse.[219] By 1973, writes Mark J. Perry from the University of Michigan, a newly built U.S. home averaged 1,660 square feet. In 2017, it averaged 2,631 square feet. That's a 59 percent improvement. Over the same period, the size of the average U.S. household fell from 3.01 to 2.54 people. As such, the living space of an average American increased from 551 square feet in 1973 to 1,058 square feet in 2017.[220] That amounts to an average increase in living space per person of 92 percent.

Between 1973 and 2017, the share of new houses built with four or more bedrooms rose from 23 percent to 46 percent. Moreover, the share of houses with three or more bathrooms rose from 12 percent to 37 percent between 1987 and 2017.[221]

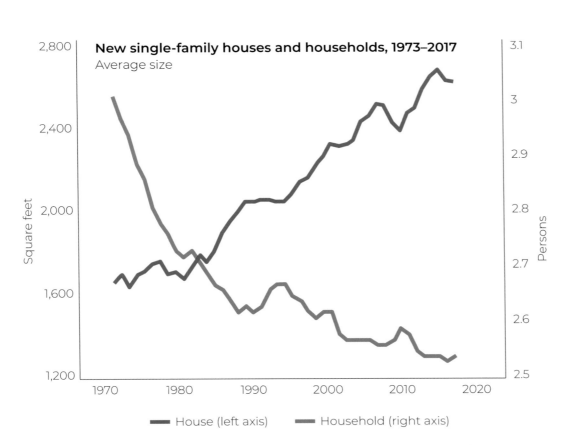

New single-family houses and households, 1973–2017
Average size

Source: Mark J. Perry, personal communication with author (Marian L. Tupy), July 2, 2018.

RISING VACCINATION AND PLUNGING INFECTIOUS DISEASE

Vaccines are among the most effective healthcare innovations ever devised. A November 2013 *New England Journal of Medicine* article—which drew on the University of Pittsburgh's Project Tycho database of infectious disease statistics since 1888—concludes that vaccinations have prevented 103 million cases of polio, measles, rubella, mumps, hepatitis A, diphtheria, and pertussis since 1924.[222] According to Dr. Donald S. Burke, a coauthor of the study, over

> **"The Centers for Disease Control and Prevention reports that before the vaccine era, nearly all children got measles by the time they were 15 years old. In the United States, the disease infected 3 million to 4 million people, hospitalizing 48,000 and killing between 400 and 500 each year."**

the past century, vaccination has likely prevented deaths of between 3 million and 4 million Americans, and has greatly reduced hospitalization rates and the sheer misery of illness.

The Centers for Disease Control and Prevention reports that before the vaccine era, nearly all children got measles by the time they were 15 years old. In the United States, the disease infected 3 million to 4 million people, hospitalizing 48,000 and killing between 400 and 500 each year.

In the prevaccine era, the annual infection rate of pertussis (whooping cough) was 817 per 100,000, mostly children under 5 years old, averaging about 7,300 deaths per year.

In the early 1950s, before a vaccine was licensed, the number of paralytic poliomyelitis cases averaged 24,000 annually and resulted in 1,500 deaths per year. The last case of polio originating in the United States was in 1979. The chart on the right shows the rate of infections before and after vaccines for pertussis, polio, measles, mumps, rubella, and hepatitis A were introduced.[223]

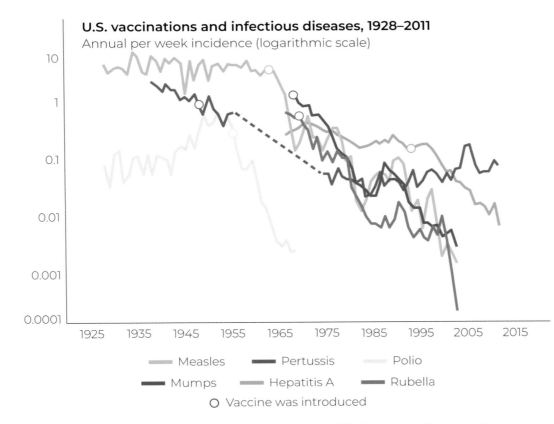

U.S. vaccinations and infectious diseases, 1928–2011

Annual per week incidence (logarithmic scale)

Legend:
— Measles — Pertussis — Polio
— Mumps — Hepatitis A — Rubella
○ Vaccine was introduced

AIR TRAVEL IS GETTING CHEAPER

The Airline Deregulation Act of 1978 began a process of liberalization of American air travel, which culminated in the dissolution of the Civil Aeronautics Board, a federal agency charged with setting the flight routes and fares of American airlines between 1939 and 1985.

Before deregulation, when they could not compete with one another by

> **"Consequently, flying was effectively restricted to the very rich. In 1955, to give a couple of examples, Trans World Airlines—a major American airline between 1930 and 2001—advertised one-way tickets from Boston to Los Angeles and from Pittsburgh to San Francisco for $1,000 and $907, respectively (figures are in 2018 dollars)."**

lowering their fares or by encroaching on each other's territory, airlines competed on service alone. Back then, flying was a glamorous affair.

It was characterized by plentiful food and drink, beautifully bedecked staff, and no extra charges. Today, it is fondly remembered as the "golden age of aviation." Consequently, flying was effectively restricted to the very rich. In 1955, to give a couple of examples, Trans World Airlines—a major American airline between 1930 and 2001—advertised one-way tickets from Boston to Los Angeles and from Pittsburgh to San Francisco for $1,000 and $907, respectively (figures are in 2018 dollars). In the fall of 2018, Spirit Airlines offered the former route for $105 and the latter route for $137.

Spirit, Frontier Airlines, JetBlue, and Southwest Airlines are a new breed of low-cost carriers. They arose after deregulation and specialize in no-frills mass transport that has democratized air travel. According to data compiled by Mark J. Perry from the University of Michigan at Flint, the average round-trip U.S. domestic airfare with fees fell from $631 in 1979 to $363 in 2017 (figures are in 2017 dollars). That's a reduction of 43 percent.

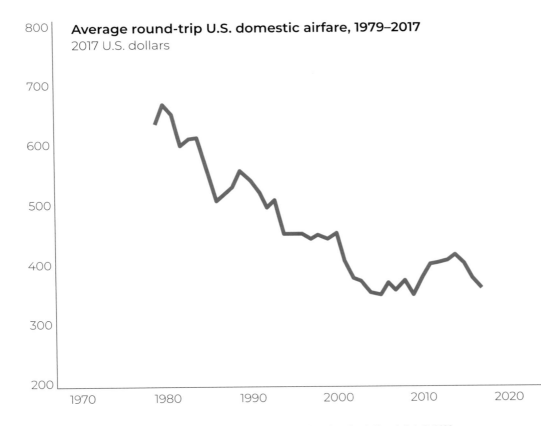

Average round-trip U.S. domestic airfare, 1979–2017
2017 U.S. dollars

Source: Mark J. Perry, personal communication with author (Marian L. Tupy), July 2, 2018.

CANCER INCIDENCE AND DEATH RATES AT 26-YEAR LOW

"The cancer death rate rose until 1991, then fell continuously through 2017, resulting in an overall decline of 29 percent that translates into an estimated 2.9 million fewer cancer deaths than would have occurred if peak rates had persisted," notes the American Cancer Society (ACS) in its annual cancer mortality and incidence statistics update in 2020.[224] In 1991, the cancer death rate stood at 215 per 100,000 people. That fell to 152 per 100,000 people in 2017.

> **"The reduction in death rates for breast, prostate, and colorectal cancer reflect the use of screening tests that result in earlier detection and, in the case of colorectal cancer, the removal of precancerous polyps during colonoscopy."**

The report also notes that the cancer death rate between 2008 and 2017 . declined at a rate of 1.5 percent per year.

In addition, the ACS reports that the cancer incidence rate decline has recently stabilized due in part to a slowing decrease in colorectal cancer rates for males and a slight uptick in breast cancer among women.

In other words, the modern world is not experiencing a rising epidemic of cancer, but rather the opposite.

Most of the decline in both incidence and mortality rates is due to reduction in smoking tobacco, as well as advances in the early detection and treatment of cancer. According to the ACS report, lung cancer death rates dropped by 51 percent among men between 1990 and 2017. They fell by 26 percent among women between 2002 and 2017.

Moreover, breast cancer death rates dropped by 40 percent among women between 1989 and 2017; prostate cancer death rates dropped by 52 percent between 1993 and 2017; and colorectal cancer death rates dropped by 54 percent among both men and women between 1970 and 2017.

The reduction in death rates for breast, prostate, and colorectal cancer reflect the use of screening tests that result in earlier detection and, in the case of colorectal cancer, the removal of precancerous polyps during colonoscopy.

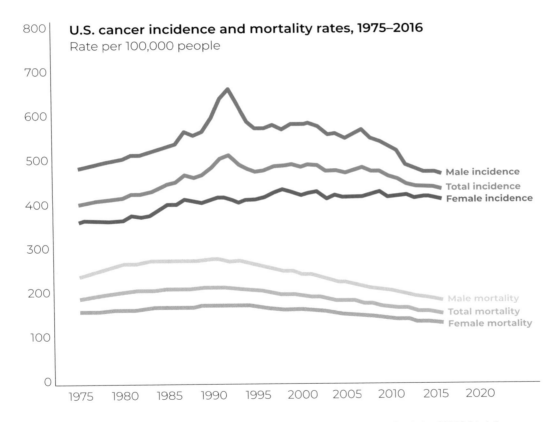

U.S. cancer incidence and mortality rates, 1975–2016

Rate per 100,000 people

Male incidence
Total incidence
Female incidence

Male mortality
Total mortality
Female mortality

Source: Rebecca L. Siegel, Kimberly D. Miller, and Ahmedin Jemal, "Cancer Statistics, 2020," *CA: A Cancer Journal for Clinicians* 70, no. 1 (January/February 2020): 15, Figure 2.

ACKNOWLEDGMENTS

We first want to acknowledge the immense intellectual debt that we owe to Julian Simon, whose groundbreaking research conclusively demonstrated how human ingenuity over the long term enables both people and the natural world to thrive together.

We wish to thank Kim Dennis, Richard Tren, Gerard Alexander, and Courtney Myers at the Searle Freedom Trust for their belief in this project and the generous support they arranged for researching and writing this book. We are also grateful to the Cato Institute for publishing it. Andrew Forrester did a sterling job curating the data, and Jason Kuznicki provided excellent editorial advice.

Marian L. Tupy wishes to thank his summer 2018 interns, Emily Johnson and Taylor Sutton, and Ian Vásquez for time from office duties. Finally, he wishes to thank Steven Pinker, Mark J. Perry, and Branko Milanovic for sharing their data with the authors.

Ronald Bailey thanks Katherine Mangu-Ward, David Nott, Nick Gillespie, Matt Welch, and Virginia Postrel at *Reason* for providing the best intellectual home any journalist could desire. It's a fun place to work too. In addition, he is indebted to the folks at the Property Environment Research Center, especially Terry Anderson, Bobby McCormick, and Reed Watson, for deepening Ron's understanding of the crucial interactions between the environment, markets, and bureaucracy. Although they have not always agreed, Fred Smith at the Competitive Enterprise Institute has greatly helped Ron to sharpen the latter's thinking on public policy, especially with respect to the problems stemming from government failure.

Last but not least, we wish to thank the Cato Institute's Eleanor O'Connor for shepherding this book through the publishing process and Guillermina Sutter Schneider and Luis Ahumada Abrigo for countless hours they spent designing this book to make it look as beautiful as it does.

NOTES

1   Milan Dinic, "Is the World Getting Better or Worse?," *YouGov Daily*, January 8, 2016.

2   Steven Pinker, "Enlightenment Wars: Some Reflections on 'Enlightenment Now,' One Year Later," *Quillette*, January 14, 2019.

3   Johan Galtung and Mari Holmboe Ruge, "The Structure of Foreign News: The Presentation of the Congo, Cuba and Cyprus Crises in Four Norwegian Newspapers," *Journal of Peace Research 2*, no. 1 (1965): 69.

4   Amos Tversky and Daniel Kahneman, "Availability: A Heuristic for Judging Frequency and Probability," *Cognitive Psychology 5*, no. 2 (1973): 207.

5   Peter Reuell, "New Research by Daniel Gilbert Speaks to Our Conflicted Relationship with Progress," *Harvard Gazette*, June 28, 2018.

6   Oliver Burkeman, "Is the World Really Better Than Ever?," *The Guardian*, July 28, 2017.

7   Daron Acemoglu and James A. Robinson, *Why Nations Fail: The Origins of Power, Prosperity, and Poverty* (New York: Crown Business, 2012), p. 96.

8   Acemoglu and Robinson, *Why Nations Fail*, p. 430.

9   Angus Maddison, *The World Economy: A Millennial Perspective* (Paris: Organisation for Economic Co-operation and Development, 2001), Table B-18. Table was adjusted from 1990 constant dollars to 2011 constant dollars.

10   World Bank, "Global Gross Domestic Product, Purchasing Power Parity" chart, https://data.worldbank.org/indicator/NY.GDP.MKTP.PP.KD.

11   Rob Dellink et al., "Long-Term Economic Growth Projections in the Shared Socioeconomic Pathways," *Global Environmental Change* 42 (2017): 206.

12   Calculated averaging World Bank annual global GDP growth rates since 2001 at https://data.worldbank.org/indicator/NY.GDP.MKTP.KD.ZG.

13   François Bourguignon and Christian Morrisson, "Inequality among World Citizens: 1820–1992," *American Economic Review* 92, no. 4 (2002): 731.

14   World Bank, "Poverty Headcount Ratio" chart, https://data.worldbank.org/topic/poverty.

15   World Bank, *Poverty and Shared Prosperity 2018: Piecing Together the Poverty Puzzle* (Washington: World Bank, 2018), Table O.1, p. 8.

16   Paul R. Ehrlich, *The Population Bomb* (New York: Ballantine Books, 1968), p. 172.

17   Gale L. Pooley and Marian L. Tupy, "The Simon Abundance Index: A New Way to Measure Availability of Resources," Cato Policy Analysis no. 857, December 4, 2018.

18   Pooley and Tupy, "Simon Abundance Index."

19   Wolfgang Lutz et al., eds., "Demographic and Human Capital Scenarios for the 21st Century: 2018 Assessment for 201 Countries," European Commission Joint Research Centre, 2018, p. 8.

20   Lutz et al., "Demographic and Human Capital Scenarios."

21   UN Department of Economic and Social Affairs, *World Population Prospects 2019: Highlights* (New York: United Nations, 2019), p. 1.

22   Frank Dikötter, "Mao's Great Leap to Famine," *New York Times*, opinion, December 15, 2010.

23   FAOSTAT, Food Balance Sheets website, UN Food and Agriculture Organization, January 27, 2020, http://www.fao.org/faostat/en/#search/ Food%20supply%20kcal%2Fcapita%2Fday.

24   FAOSTAT, Food Balance Sheets website.

25   Ehrlich, *Population Bomb*, p. 11.

26   Xiao-Peng Song et al., "Global Land Change from 1982 to 2016," *Nature* 560, no. 1 (2018): 639.

27   Peter B. Reich, "Biogeochemistry: Taking Stock of Forest Carbon," *Nature Climate Change* 1, no. 7 (2011): 346.

28   United Nations, "World Deforestation Slows Down as More Forests Are Better Managed," UN Food and Agriculture Organization, September 7, 2015.

29   Carolyn Dimitri, Anne Effland, and Neilson Conklin, "The 20th Century Transformation of U.S. Agriculture and Farm Policy," Economic Information Bulletin no. 3, Economic Research Service, U.S. Department of Agriculture, June 1, 2005, p. 2.

30   World Bank, *World Development Report 2009: Reshaping Economic Geography* (Washington: World Bank, 2009), p. 24.

31   United Nations, "68% of the World Population Projected to Live in Urban Areas by 2050, Says UN," Department of Economic and Social Affairs, United Nations, May 16, 2018.

32   Organisation for Economic Co-operation and Development (OECD), "The Metropolitan Century: Understanding Urbanisation and its Consequences, Policy Highlights," OECD Publishing, 2015, https://www.oecd.org/regional/regional-policy/The-Metropolitan-Century-Policy-Highlights%20.pdf

33   Francis Fukuyama, "Have We Reached the End of History?," RAND Corporation, Santa Monica, CA, 1989, p. 1.

34   Monty G. Marshall and Gabrielle Elzinga-Marshall, "Global Report 2017: Conflict, Governance, and State Fragility," Center for Systemic Peace, Vienna, VA, August 27, 2017.

35   Thomas S. Szayna et al., "What Are the Trends in Armed Conflicts, and What Do They Mean for U.S. Defense Policy?," RAND Corporation, Santa Monica, CA, 2017, p. 1

36   Stephan De Spiegeleire, Khrystyna Holynska, and Yevhen Sapolovych, "Things May Not Be as They Seem: Geo-Dynamic Trends in the International System," in *Strategic Monitor* 2018–2019, eds., Tim Sweijs and Danny Pronk (The Hague: Clingendael Institute, 2019), Figure 10.

37   Centre for Research on the Epidemiology of Disasters, Emergency Events Database (EM-DAT) website, 2019, https://www.emdat.be/.

38   Centre for Research on the Epidemiology of Disasters (CRED) and United Nations Office for Disaster Risk Reduction (UNISDR), "Poverty and Death: Disaster Mortality, 1996–2015," 2016, p. 112, https://reliefweb.int/sites/reliefweb.int/files/resources/CRED_Disaster_Mortality.pdf.

39   CRED and UNISDR, "Poverty and Death," p. 3.

40   Roger Pielke, "Tracking Progress on the Economic Costs of Disasters under the Indicators of the Sustainable Development Goals," *Environmental Hazards* 18, no. 1 (2019): 1–6.

41   UN Development Programme, Human Development Reports, 2018, Table 2, http://hdr.undp.org/en/composite/trends.

42   World Values Survey, "Wave 7," WVS online data analysis, http://www.worldvaluessurvey.org/WVSOnline.jsp.

43   Ronald F. Inglehart, *Cultural Evolution: People's Motivations Are Changing, and Reshaping the World* (Cambridge: Cambridge University Press, 2018), p. 156.

44   Inglehart, *Cultural Evolution*, pp. 218–20.

45   Branko Milanovic, "Global Income Inequality in Numbers: In History and Now," *Global Policy Volume 4*, no. 2 (May 2013): 198–208.

46   World Bank, "Population Living in Slums" chart, https://data.worldbank.org/indicator/EN.POP.SLUM.UR.ZS?locations=ZG-1W-8SZ4-ZJ.

47   UN-Habitat, *World Cities Report 2016: Urbanization and Development—Emerging Futures* (Nairobi: UN-Habitat, 2016).

48   Our World in Data, "Share of Countries Having Achieved Different Milestones in Women's Political Representation" chart, 2017, https:// ourworldindata.org/grapher/political-representation-of-women?time=1907.

49   A. W. Geiger and Lauren Kent, "Number of Women Leaders around the World Has Grown, but They're Still a Small Group," Pew Research Center, March 8, 2017.

50   World Bank, "Proportion of Seats Held by Women in National Parliaments" chart, https://data.worldbank.org/indicator/SG.GEN.PARL.ZS.

51   Ronald Lee, "The Demographic Transition: Three Centuries of Fundamental Change," *Journal of Economic Perspectives* 17, no. 4 (2003): 168.

52   Nicola L. Bulled and Richard Sosis, "Examining the Relationship between Life Expectancy, Reproduction, and Educational Attainment," *Human Nature* 21, no. 3 (2010): 276

53   Luis Crouch and Silvia Montoya, "Measuring Functional Literacy and Numeracy for Lifelong Learning," Data for Sustainable Development (blog), November 11, 2017.

54   UNESCO, *Education for People and Planet: Creating Sustainable Futures for All, Global Education Monitoring Report 2016* (Paris: UNESCO, 2016), p. 53.

55   World Bank, "Literacy Rate, Adult Total" chart, https://data.worldbank.org/indicator/SE.ADT.LITR.ZS.

56   World Bank, "School Enrollment, Primary" chart, https://data.worldbank.org/indicator/SE.PRM.ENRR?end=2017&locations=1W&start=1970.

57   World Bank, "School Enrollment, Secondary" chart, https://data.worldbank.org/indicator/ SE.SEC.ENRR?end=2017&locations=1W&start=1970.

58   World Bank, "School Enrollment, Tertiary" chart, https://data.worldbank.org/indicator/ SE.TER.ENRR?end=2017&locations=1W&start=1970.

59   George Psacharopoulos and Harry Anthony Patrinos, "Returns to Investment in Education: A Decennial Review of the Global Literature," *Education Economics* 26, no. 5 (2018): 445, http://datatopics.worldbank.org/education/files/GlobalAchievement/ ReturnsInteractive.pdf.

60   Robert Barro and Jong-Wha Lee, Educational Attainment Dataset website, http://www.barrolee.com/.

61   Robert Barro and Jong-Wha Lee, "Educational Attainment for Total Population, 1950–2010," June 2018 update, http://www.barrolee.com/.

62   Kyle J. Foreman et al., "Forecasting Life Expectancy, Years of Life Lost, and All-Cause and Cause-Specific Mortality for 250 Causes of Death: Reference and Alternative Scenarios for 2016–40 for 195 Countries and Territories," *The Lancet* 392, no. 10159 (2018): 2053–90 .

63   James R. Flynn, "The Mean IQ of Americans: Massive Gains 1932 to 1978," *Psychological Bulletin* 95, no. 1 (1984): 29–51.

64   Jakob Pietschnig and Martin Voracek, "One Century of Global IQ Gains: A Formal Meta-Analysis of the Flynn Effect (1909–2013)," *Perspectives on Psychological Science* 10, no. 3 (2015): 285.

65   Bernt Bratsberg and Ole Rogeberg, "Flynn Effect and Its Reversal Are Both Environmentally Caused," *Proceedings of the National Academy of Sciences* 115, no. 26 (2018): 6674–78.

66   James R. Flynn and Michael Shayer, "IQ Decline and Piaget: Does the Rot Start at the Top?," *Intelligence* 66 (2018): 1.

67   Lucas Ramón Mendos, *State Sponsored Homophobia*, 13th ed. (Geneva: International Lesbian, Gay, Bisexual, Trans and Intersex Association, 2019), dataset, https://ilga.org/state-sponsored-homophobia-report.

68   Freedom House, *Freedom of the Press 2006: A Global Survey of Media Independence* (Lanham, MD: Rowman & Littlefield, 2006.

69   Freedom House, "Freedom of the Press 2017: Press Freedom's Dark Horizon," 2017, https://freedomhouse.org/report/ freedom-press/freedompress-2017.

70   World Bank, "Life Expectancy at Birth" chart, https://data.worldbank.org/indicator/sp.dyn.le00.in.

71   World Bank, "Life Expectancy at Birth: United States" chart, https://data.worldbank.org/indicator/SP.DYN.LE00.IN?locations=US.

72   UN Population Division, *World Population Prospects: Key Findings & Advance Tables,* 2017 Revision, vol. 2 (New York: United Nations, 2017), p. 37.

73   U.S. Census Bureau, "QuickFacts: United States," https://www.census.gov/quickfacts/fact/table/US/PST045218.

74   David M. Cutler and Ellen Meara, "Changes in the Age Distribution of Mortality over the 20th Century," National Bureau of Economic Research Working Paper no. 8556, October, 2001, p. 44.

75   Victoria Hansen et al., "Infectious Disease Mortality Trends in the United States, 1980–2014," *Journal of the American Medical Association* 316, no. 20 (2016): 2149.

76   World Bank, "Death Rate, Crude" chart, https://data.worldbank.org/indicator/sp.dyn.cdrt.in?end=2016.

77   Olga Basso, "Reproductive Epidemiology in an Evolutionary Perspective: Why Bigger May Not Be Better," *Current Epidemiological Reports* 1, no 2 (2014): 98.

78   World Health Organization (WHO), "Sustainable Development Goal 3: Health: Ensure Healthy Lives and Promote Wellbeing for All at All Ages," https:// www.who.int/topics/sustainable-development-goals/targets/en/.

79   WHO, "Health Statistics and Information Systems: Maternal Mortality Ratio," 2019, https://www.who.int/healthinfo/ statistics/indmaternalmortality/en/.

80   WHO, Health statistics and information systems, "Maternal Mortality Ratio (per 100,000 Live Births)," https://www.who.int/healthinfo/statistics/indmaternalmortality/en/.

81   WHO, "10 Facts on Immunization," March 2018 update, http://origin.who.int/features/factfiles/immunization/en/.

82   James Gallagher, "AIDS: Origin of Pandemic 'Was 1920s Kinshasa,'" BBC News, October 3, 2014.

83   UNAIDS, Global Aids Monitoring 2020, December 24, 2019, https://www.unaids.org/en/global-aids-monitoring.

84   United Nations Development Programme, "World AIDS Day: Record Drop in Cost of HIV Treatment," November 30, 2015, https:// www.undp.org/content/undp/en/home/presscenter/articles/2015/11/30/world-aids-day-record-drop-in-cost-of-hiv-treatment.html.

85   WHO, "Tuberculosis" fact sheet, September 18, 2018, https://www.who.int/news-room/fact-sheets/detail/tuberculosis.

86   World Bank, *World Development Indicators*, "Incidence of Tuberculosis (per 100,000 People)" chart, https://data.worldbank.org/indicator/SH.TBS.INCD.

87   World Bank, *World Development Indicators*, "Tuberculosis Case Detection Rate (%, All Forms)" chart, https://data.worldbank.org/indicator/SH.TBS.DTEC.ZS.

88   World Bank, *World Development Indicators*, "Tuberculosis Treatment Success Rate (% of New Cases)" chart, https://data.worldbank.org/indicator/SH.TBS.CURE.ZS.

89   Tuoyo Okorosobo et al., "Economic Burden of Malaria in Six Countries of Africa," *European Journal of Business and Management* 3, no. 6 (2011): 43.

90   Institute for Health Metrics and Evaluation, "GBD Results Tool; Location: Global; Year: 1990–2017; Cause; Age: All Ages; Metric: Number; Measure: Deaths; Sex: Both; Cause: A.4.1 Malaria," Global Burden of Disease Study results, 2017, http://ghdx.healthdata.org/gbd-results-tool.

91   WHO, "Cancer" fact sheet, September 12, 2018, https://www.who.int/en/news-room/fact-sheets/detail/cancer.

92   Max Roser and Hannah Ritchie, "Cancer," Our World in Data, April 2018 update, https://ourworldindata.org/cancer.

93   Our World in Data, "Cancer Death Rates" map, 2017, https://ourworldindata.org/grapher/cancer-death-rates.

94   Max Roser and Hannah Ritchie, "Smoking," Our World in Data, 2019, https://ourworldindata.org/smoking.

95   Manuel Eisner, "Long-Term Historical Trends in Violent Crime," *Crime and Justice* 30 (2003): 83–142.

96   Institute for Health Metrics and Evaluation, "GBD Results Tool; Measure: Deaths and DALYs; Age: All Ages; Year: 2017; Cause: Total All Causes; Location: Global; Sex: Both; Metric: Number, Percent, and Rate," Global Burden of Disease Study results, 2018, http://ghdx.healthdata.org/gbdresults-tool.

97   Steven Pinker, personal communication with author (Marian L. Tupy), August 18, 2018.

98   Amnesty International, "Death Penalty in 2018: Facts and Figures," April 10, 2019, https://www.amnesty.org/en/latest/news/2019/04/deathpenalty-facts-and-figures-2018/.

99   UN Sustainable Development Solutions Network, "SDG16 Data Initiative: 2018 Global Report," July 2018, p. 5.

100   Bjarne Røsjø, "The Long Peace Most Likely Began during the Vietnam War," Conflict Patterns, Peace Research, Regions and Powers, *PRIO Blogs*, June 6, 2018, https://blogs.prio.org/2018/06/the-long-peace-most-likely-began-during-the-vietnam-war/.

101   Frank Chalk and Kurt Jonassohn, quoted in Steven Pinker's *The Better Angels of Our Nature: Why Violence Has Declined*, (New York: Penguin Books, 2011), p. 333.

102   UN Office on Genocide Prevention and the Responsibility to Protect, "Definitions: Genocide," https://www.un.org/en/genocideprevention/genocide.shtml.

103   Uppsala University, "Recorded Fatalities in UCDP Organized Violence 1989–2017," UCPD Conflict Encyclopedia, https://ucdp.uu.se/.

104   Steven Pinker, "Has the Decline of Violence Reversed since The Better Angels of Our Nature Was Written?," Steven Pinker.com, 2017.

105   World Bank, "Military Expenditure" chart, https://data.worldbank.org/indicator/MS.MIL.XPND.GD.ZS?end=2017&locations=ZG-1W-XU-ZJZ7-8S-Z4-ZQ&start=1960.

106   Stockholm International Peace Research Institute, "Global Military Spending Remains High at $1.7 Trillion" chart, May 2, 2018, https://www.sipri.org/media/press-release/2018/global-military-spending-remains-high-17-trillion.

107   Pinker, *Better Angels of Our Nature*, p. 210.

108   Council on Foreign Relations, Global Conflict Tracker website, https://www.cfr.org/interactive/global-conflict-tracker/?category=us.

109   Atomic Archive, "The Atomic Bombings of Hiroshima and Nagasaki," http://www.atomicarchive.com/Docs/MED/med_chp10.shtml.

110   Joseph Cirincione, "Lessons Lost," *Bulletin of the Atomic Scientists* 61, no. 6 (2005): 47.

111   Gregory Clark, *A Farewell to Alms: A Brief Economic History of the World* (Princeton, NJ: Princeton University Press, 2008), p. 68.

112   Andorra, Antigua and Barbuda, Argentina, Aruba, Australia, Austria, Bahamas, Bahrain, Barbados, Belgium, Bermuda, British Virgin Islands, Brunei Darussalam, Canada, Cayman Islands, Channel Islands, Chile, Croatia, Curaçao, Cyprus, Czech Republic, Denmark, Estonia, Faroe Islands, Finland, France, French Polynesia, Germany, Gibraltar, Greece, Greenland, Guam, Hong Kong SAR, Hungary,

Iceland, Ireland, Isle of Man, Israel, Italy, Japan, Kuwait, Latvia, Liechtenstein, Lithuania, Luxembourg, Macao SAR, Malta, Monaco, Netherlands, New Caledonia, New Zealand, Northern Mariana Islands, Norway, Oman, Palau, Panama, Poland, Portugal, Puerto Rico, Qatar, Saint Martin (French side), San Marino, Saudi Arabia, Seychelles, Singapore, Sint Maarten (Dutch side), Slovak Republic, Slovenia, South Korea, Spain, St. Kitts and Nevis, Sweden, Switzerland, Taiwan, Trinidad and Tobago, Turks and Caicos Islands, United Arab Emirates, United Kingdom, United States, Uruguay, and U.S. Virgin Islands.

113   Authors' calculation based on data from the Conference Board, Total Economy Database—Key Findings, April 2019, https://www.conference-board.org/data/economydatabase.

114   OSHAcademy, "Agriculture: Agricultural Safety," https://www.oshatrain.org/pages/agricultural_safety.html.

115   Päivi Hämäläinen, Jukka Takala, and Tan Boon Kiat, *Global Estimates of Occupational Accidents and Work-Related Illnesses 2017* (Singapore: Workplace Safety and Health Institute, 2017), p. 8.

116   Steven Pinker, *Enlightenment Now: The Case for Reason, Science, Humanism, and Progress* (New York: Penguin Books, 2018), p. 185.

117   Pinker, *Enlightenment Now*, p. 187.

118   Hämäläinen, Takala, and Kiat, *Global Estimates of Occupational Accidents*, p. 11.

119   Johan Norberg, *Progress: Ten Reasons to Look Forward to the Future* (London: Oneworld, 2016), p. 191.

120   Esteban Ortiz-Ospina and Max Roser, "Child Labor," Our World in Data, 2019, https://ourworldindata.org/child-labor.

121   National Institute of Food and Agriculture, "Growing a Nation: An Interactive Timeline of the History of Agriculture in the United States," 2014, https://www.agclassroom.org/gan/timeline/farmers_land.htm.

122   World Bank, "Employment in Agriculture" chart, April 2019, https://data.worldbank.org/indicator/sl.agr.empl.zs.

123   Charles Hirschman and Elizabeth Mogford, "Immigration and the American Industrial Revolution from 1880 to 1920," *Social Science Research* 38, no. 4 (2009): 30.

124   Federal Reserve Bank of St. Louis, "All Employees: Manufacturing/All Employees: Total Nonfarm Payrolls" chart, 2019, https://fred.stlouisfed.org/graph/?g=cAYh.

125   Donald M. Fisk, "American Labor in the 20th Century," U.S. Bureau of Labor Statistics, Compensation and Working Conditions, Fall 2001, p. 1.

126   U.S. Bureau of Labor Statistics, "Employment by Major Industry Sector" table, 2006, 2016, and projected 2026, https://www.bls.gov/emp/tables/ employment-by-major-industry-sector.htm.

127   World Bank, "Employment in Industry" chart, April 2019, https://data.worldbank.org/indicator/SL.IND.EMPL.ZS?locations=BD-CN-IN-VN.

128   Hämäläinen, Takala, and Kiat, *Global Estimates of Occupational Accidents*, p. 8.

129   World Economic Forum, *The Global Gender Gap Report 2018* (Geneva: World Economic Forum, 2018), p. viii.

130   Jonathan Haidt, "How Capitalism Changes Conscience," Center for Humans and Nature, September 28, 2015, https://www.humansandnature.org/culture-how-capitalism-changes-conscience.

131   OECD, "Gender Wage Gap" chart, 2019, https://data.oecd.org/earnwage/gender-wagegap.htm.

132   OECD, "Gender Wage Gap" chart.

133   Andrew Chamberlain, "Demystifying the Gender Pay Gap: Evidence from Glassdoor Salary Data," Glassdoor Inc., March 2016.

134   Steven Pinker, personal communication with author (Marian L. Tupy), July 16, 2018.

135   Jesse H. Ausubel, "Peak Farmland and Potatoes" (plenary address, 2014 Potato Business Summit of the United Potato Growers of America, San Antonio, TX, January 8, 2014), p. 6.

136   UN Food and Agriculture Organization, "Land Use," FAO Stat, http://www.fao.org/faostat/en/#data/RL/visualize.

137   Jesse H. Ausubel, Iddo K. Wernick, and Paul E. Waggoner, "Peak Farmland and the Prospect for Land Sparing," *Population and Development Review* 38 (2012): 237.

138   Protected Planet, *World Database on Protected Areas*, https://www.protectedplanet.net/c/world-database-on-protected-areas.

139   UN Environment World Conservation Monitoring Centre, International Union for the Conservation of Nature, and National Geographic Society, *Protected Planet Report 2018: Tracking Progress towards Global Targets for Protected Areas* (Cambridge: UNEP-WC-MC, 2018), pp. 1–56.

140   World Bank, "CO2 Emissions" chart, https://data.worldbank.org/indicator/EN.ATM.CO2E.KD.GD?locations=US-CN-1W-8S-EU.

141   Kenneth S. Deffeyes, *Beyond Oil: The View from Hubbert's Peak* (New York: Strauss and Giroux, 2005), p. 3.

142   BP plc, "Statistical Review of World Energy 2019," June 2019, https://www.bp.com/en/global/corporate/energy-economics/statistical-review-of-world-energy.html.

143   BP plc, "Statistical Review of World Energy 2019," June 2019, https://www.bp.com/en/global/corporate/energy-economics/statistical-review-of-world-energy.html.

144   U.S. Energy Information Administration, International data, "Crude Oil Including Lease Condensate," http://www.eia.doe.gov/emeu/international/oilreserves.html.

145   Mary Fagan, "Sheikh Yamani Predicts Price Crash as Age of Oil Ends," *The Telegraph*, June 25, 2000.

146   UN Food and Agriculture Organization, "Water Withdrawal by Sector, around 2010" table, November 2016, https://www.globalagriculture.org/ fileadmin/files/weltagrarbericht/Weltagrarbericht/13Wasser/2016WorldData-Withdrawal_eng.pdf.

147   Rowan Jacobsen, "Israel Proves the Desalination Era Is Here," *Ensia*, July 29, 2016, reprinted in *Scientific American*, https://www.scientificamerican.com/article/israel-proves-the-desalination-era-is-here/.

148   World Bank, *World Development Indicators*, "Water Productivity, Total (Constant 2010 US$ GDP per Cubic Meter of Total Freshwater Withdrawal" chart, https://data.worldbank.org/indicator/ER.GDP.FWTL.M3.KD.

149   Jesse H. Ausubel and Paul E. Waggoner, "Dematerialization: Variety, Caution, and Persistence," *Proceedings of the National Academy of Sciences* 105, no. 35 (2008): 12774 .

150   Arnulf Grubler et al., "A Low Energy Demand Scenario for Meeting the 1.5 °C Target and Sustainable Development Goals without Negative Emission Technologies," *Nature Energy* 3, no. 1 (2018): 515–27. Arnulf Grubler was kind enough to give us his permission to republish his graphic in this book. The original graphic appeared in World in 2050 Initiative, *The Digital Revolution and Sustainable Development: Opportunities and Challenges* (Laxenburg, Austria: International Institute for Applied Systems Analysis, 2019).

151   Robert Conquest, *The Harvest of Sorrow: Soviet Civilization and the Terror-Famine* (New York: Oxford University Press, 1986), pp. 300–307.

152   Frank Dikötter, *Mao's Great Famine: The History of China's Most Devastating Catastrophe, 1958–1962* (London: Bloomsbury Publishing, 2010), pp. 298, 325.

153   International Potato Center, "Facts and Figures about the Potato," 2017, https://nkxms1019hx1xmtstxk3k9sko-wpengine.netdna-ssl.com/wpcontent/uploads/2017/04/Facts-and-Figures-Potato-Eng-2017.pdf.

154   World Bank, "Cereal Production" chart, https://data.worldbank.org/indicator/AG.PRD.CREL.MT?view=chart.

155   UN Food and Agriculture Organization, "Land Use" webpage, http://www.fao.org/faostat/en/#data/RL.

156   Helen Goodchild, "Modelling Roman Demography and Urban Dependency in Central Italy," *Theoretical Roman Archaeology Journal* (2005): 44.

157   Alexander Apostolides et al., "English Agricultural Output and Labor Productivity, 1250–1850: Some Preliminary Estimates," Warwick University Working Paper, November 26, 2008.

158   Paul Brassley, "Output and Technical Change in Twentieth-Century British Agriculture," *Agricultural History Review* 48, no. 1 (2000): 66.

159   U.S. Department of Agriculture, "Crop Production Historical Track Records," April 2018, pp. 28–30.

160   Jack A. Goldstone, "Feeding the People, Starving the State: China's Agricultural Revolution of the 17th/18th Centuries," School of Public Policy, George Mason University, September 2003.

161   Ricepedia, "China," http://ricepedia.org/china.

162   UK Department for Environment, Food and Rural Affairs, "Farming Statistics: Provisional Crop Areas, Yields and Livestock Populations at June 2018–United Kingdom," October 11, 2018, p. 11.

163   U.S. Department of Agriculture, "Crop Production: 2018 Summary," February 2019, p. 11.

164   Nathan Childs and Sharon Raszap, "U.S. 2018/19 Crop Estimate Raised 3 Percent to 224.2 Million Cwt," Rice Outlook, February 12, 2019, p. 8.

165   Ricepedia, "China."

166   World Bank, "Cereal Yield" chart, https://data.worldbank.org/indicator/ag.yld.crel.kg.

167   UN Food and Agriculture Organization, "World Review of Fisheries and Aquaculture," Part 1, Figure 1, http://www.fao.org/3/X8002E/x8002e04.htm.

168   UN Food and Agriculture Organization, *The State of World Fisheries and Aquaculture 2018: Meeting the Sustainable Development Goals* (Rome: FAO, 2018), p. 13.

169   UN Food and Agriculture Organization, *State of World Fisheries and Aquaculture 2018*, p. 17.

170   Jelle Bruinsma, ed., *World Agriculture: Towards 2015/2030, An FAO Perspective* (Rome: FAO, 2003), pp. 29–93.

171   "More Fuel for the Food/Feed Debate: New FAO Study Indicates That Livestock Primarily Consume Foods Not Fit for Human Consumption and Meat Production Requires Less Cereals Than Generally Reported," AGA News, December 3, 2018.

172   International Energy Agency, World Energy Outlook 2004 (Paris: Organisation for Economic Co-operation and Development, 2004), p. 2 .

173   World Bank, "Access to Electricity" chart, https://data.worldbank.org/indicator/EG.ELC.ACCS.ZS?locations=8S-1W-ZG-Z4-ZQ-ZJ-XU-Z7.

174   International Energy Agency, *Energy Access Outlook 2017: From Poverty to Prosperity* (Paris: Organisation for Economic Co-operation and Development, 2017), p. 11.

175   William D. Nordhaus, "Do Real-Output and Real-Wage Measures Capture Reality? The History of Lighting Suggests Not," in *The Economics of New Goods*, eds. Timothy F. Bresnahan and Robert J. Gordon (Chicago: University of Chicago Press, 1996), p. 36, http://www.nber.org/chapters/c6064.

176   Bloomberg New Energy Finance, New Energy Outlook 2015, https://www.researchgate.net/figure/Solar-PV-power-cost-from-1977-to-2015Source-Bloomberg-New-Energy-Finance-15_fig4_321943289.

177   WHO, "Drinking-Water" fact sheet, February 7, 2018, https://www.who.int/news-room/fact-sheets/detail/drinkingwater.

178   United Nations Statistics Division, *Department of Economic and Social Affairs*, "Millennium Development Goals Indicators," http://mdgs.un.org/unsd/mdg/Data.aspx.

179   Hannah Ritchie and Max Roser, "Water Use and Sanitation," Our World in Data, 2019, https://ourworldindata.org/water-use-sanitation.

180   United Nations, "Target 7.C: Halve, by 2015, the Proportion of People without Sustainable Access to Safe Drinking Water and Basic Sanitation," Millennium Development Goals, http://mdgs.un.org/unsd/mdg/Metadata.aspx?Indicatorid=0&SeriesId=668.

181   "Motorola DynaTAC 8000x," IndustrialDesignHistory.com, Auburn University, 2011, http://www.industrialdesignhistory.com/node/142.

182   World Bank, "Mobile Cellular Subscriptions" chart, https://data.worldbank.org/indicator/IT.CEL.SETS.P2?locations=US-1W-ZG.

183   World Bank, "Mobile Cellular Subscriptions" chart.

184   World Bank, "Individuals Using the Internet" chart, https://data.worldbank.org/indicator/IT.NET.USER.ZS.

185   William B. Norton, "Internet Transit Prices: Historical and Projected," DrPeering International white paper, August 2010.

186   Computer History Museum, "1980: Seagate 5.25-Inch HDD Becomes PC Standard: Personal Computer Boosts HDD Output to New Levels of Production," Storage Engine, 2018.

187   Seagate, "Seagate Reaches 1 Terabit per Square Inch Milestone in Hard Drive Storage with New Technology Demonstration," news release, March 19, 2012, https://www.seagate.com/news/news-archive/terabit-milestone-storage-seagate-master-pr/.

188   Seagate, "Seagate Reaches 1 Terabit per Square Inch."

189   Steve's Old Computer Museum, "IBM Personal Computer (PC)," timeline, http://oldcomputers.net/ibm5150.html.

190   David Reinsel, John Gantz, and John Rydning, "Data Age 2025: The Digitization of the World from Edge to Core," IDC white paper, Seagate, November 2018, p. 3, https://www.seagate.com/files/www-content/our-story/trends/files/idc-seagate-dataage-whitepaper.pdf.

191   World Bank, "International Tourism, Number of Arrivals" chart, https://data.worldbank.org/indicator/ST.INT.ARVL?locations=XD-1W-XMXN-XT.

192   Arvind Panagariya, "Miracles and Debacles: Do Free-Trade Skeptics Have a Case?," *International Trade*, University Library of Munich, Germany, 2003, p. 2.

193   World Bank, "Tariff Rate, Applied, Weighted Mean, All Products" chart, https://data.worldbank.org/indicator/TM.TAX.MRCH.WM.AR.ZS.

194   Elaine L. Chao and Kathleen P. Utgoff, "100 Years of U.S. Consumer Spending: Data for the Nation, New York City, and Boston," U.S. Department of Labor Report 991, August 3, 2006.

195   Chao and Utgoff, "100 Years of U.S. Consumer Spending," p. 34.

196   U.S. Bureau of Labor Statistics, "Consumer Expenditures—2017," news release, September 11, 2018, https://www.bls.gov/news. release/cesan. nr0.htm.

197   Robert Dietz, "Single-Family Home Size Increases at the Start of 2018," National Association of Home Builders, May 21, 2018.

198   Tvhistory.TV, "TV Selling Prices: American TV Prices," Television History—The First 75 Years, 2013, http://www.tvhistory.tv/tv-prices. htm.

199   Amazon.com, "Sceptre E249BD-SR 24 inches 720p LED TV, True Black (2017)," price as of December 2018, https://www.amazon.com/Sceptre-inches-720p-LED-E249BD-SR/dp/B071VJ5PDH.

200   "Choose Your Frigidaire Automatic Ice Maker Refrigerator Now!" ad, *Navajo Times* (Window Rock, AZ), May 16, 1968, https://newspaperarchive. com/navajo-times-may-16-1968-p-31/.

201   HomeDepot.com, "18 Cu. Ft. Top Freezer Refrigerator in White," price as of December 2018, https://www.homedepot.com/p/Frigidaire-18-cuft-Top-Freezer-Refrigerator-in-White-FFTR1814TW/301693631.

202   "Pennys Extra Value Days" ad, Florence (SC) Morning News, May 3, 1968, https://newspaperarchive.com/florence-morning-newsmay-03-1968-p-9/; and "5,000 BTU 115-Volt Window-Mounted Mini-Compact Air Conditioner with Mechanical Controls," HomeDepot. com, price as of December 2018, https://www.homedepot.com/p/Frigidaire-5-000-BTU-115-Volt-Window-Mounted-Mini-Compact-Air-Conditioner-with-Mechanical-Controls-FFRA051WAE/308328843.

203   International Slide Rule Museum, "Electronic Slide Rule Calculators (1972–1979): The Demise of the Slide Rule Industry with Related Calculators from the Early 80's," https://www.sliderulemuseum.com/Calculators.htm.

204   SHZOP.com, "Texas Instruments TI-30X IIS 2-Line Scientific Calculator, Black with Blue Accents, price as of December 2018, https://www.shzop.com/index.php/product/texas-instruments-ti-30x-iis-2-line-scientific-calculator-black-with-blue-accents/?gclid=Cj0KCQjwocPnBRDFA RIsAJJcf95t8qp3ewNk8yMuKr8zopEuZ39ogbjppmn_tXq-zGQNxOosbrFSaNYaAiXYEALw_wcB.

205   Jimmy Maher, "The Complete History of the IBM PC, Part Two: The DOS Empire Strikes," *arsTECHNICA*, July 31, 2017.

206   Walmart.com, "SmarTab 10.1' 2in1 Windows Tablet W/ Keyboard," price as of December 2018, https://www.walmart.com/ip/SmarTab-10-12in1-Windows-Tablet-W-Keyboard/227799290.

207   Steven Horwitz and Charles A. Dana, "Inequality, Mobility, and Being Poor in America," *Social Philosophy and Policy* 2 (2015): 20, https://pdfs.semanticscholar.org/d2a7/4e4b1fd6613bb6b818d1f29b12f697e5ddad.pdf.

208   Gallup News Service, "Crime," In Depth: Topics A to Z, March 2019, https://news.gallup.com/poll/1603/crime.aspx.

209   Federal Bureau of Investigation (FBI), "Crime—National or State Level: State-by-State and National Crime Estimates by Year(s)," Uniform Crime Reporting Statistics, https:// www.ucrdatatool.gov/Search/Crime/State/StatebyState.cfm?NoVariables=Y&CFID=186339778&CFTOKEN=54363ab1690d9f66-63023AA0-BC473621-E63723CAA5404829.

210   FBI, "2017 Crime in the United States" table, 2018, https://ucr.fbi.gov/crime-in-the-u.s/2017/crime-in-the-u.s.-2017/topic-pages/tables/table-1.

211   FBI, "Crime—National or State Level."

212   Michael T. Light and Ty Miller, "Does Undocumented Immigration Increase Violent Crime?," *Criminology* 56, no. 2 (2017): 370–401.

213   Institute of Government & Public Affairs, "Principles of Equality—Schools and Interracial Marriage" chart, https://igpa.uillinois.edu/programs/ racial-attitudes#section-0.

214   Institute of Government & Public Affairs, "Principles of Equality" chart.

215   Institute of Government & Public Affairs, Trends in Racial Attitudes website, https://igpa.uillinois.edu/programs/racial-attitudes.

216   Joel M. Schwartz and Steven F. Hayward, *Air Quality in America: A Dose of Reality on Air Pollution Levels, Trends, and Health Risks* (Washington: AEI Press, 2007), p. 15.

217   Environmental Protection Agency, "Percent Change in Emissions" table, 2019, https://www.epa.gov/air-trends/air-quality-nationalsummary#air-quality-trends.

218   U.S. Environmental Protection Agency, *Our Nation's Air 2018* (website) "Comparison of Growth Areas and Emissions, 1970–2018," https://www.epa.gov/sites/production/files/2019-07/2018_baby_graphic_1970-2018.png.

219   Steve Kerch, "1900 to 2010: Evolution of the American Home Today—Fun Housing Facts," *Chicago Tribune*, June 18, 2000.

220   Mark J. Perry, personal communication with author (Marian L. Tupy), July 2, 2018. The U.S. home size figures in Trend 75 differ slightly from U.S. home size figures in Trend 70. Note that the data come from two different sources and cover two slightly different time periods.

221   U.S. Department of Commerce and U.S. Department of Housing and Urban Development, *2017 Characteristics of New Housing* (Washington: U.S. Department of Commerce, 2017).

222   Willem G. van Panhuis et al., "Contagious Diseases in the United States from 1888 to the Present," *New England Journal of Medicine* 369, no. 22 (2013): 2152–58.

223   Carl Franzen, "Vaccinations Have Prevented at Least 103 Million Cases of Contagious Disease since 1924," *The Verge*, November 30, 2013, https://www.theverge.com/2013/11/30/5160490/vaccines-prevent-at-least-103-million-cases-disease-since-1924..

224   Rebecca L. Siegel, Kimberly D. Miller, and Ahmedin Jemal, "Cancer Statistics, 2020," *CA: A Cancer Journal for Clinicians* 70, no. 1 (January/February 2020): 7–30, https://doi.org/10.3322/caac.21590.

Ronald Bailey is the award-winning science correspondent for *Reason* magazine and Reason.com and author of *The End of Doom: Environmental Renewal in the Twenty-first Century*.

Marian L. Tupy is a senior fellow at the Cato Institute's Center for Global Liberty and Prosperity, coauthor of the Simon Abundance Index, and editor of the website HumanProgress.org.

Founded in 1977, the **Cato Institute** is a public policy research foundation dedicated to broadening the parameters of policy debate to allow consideration of more options that are consistent with the principles of limited government, individual liberty, and peace. To that end, the Institute strives to achieve greater involvement of the intelligent, concerned lay public in questions of policy and the proper role of government.

The Institute is named for *Cato's Letters*, libertarian pamphlets that were widely read in the American Colonies in the early 18th century and played a major role in laying the philosophical foundation for the American Revolution.

Despite the achievement of the nation's Founders, today virtually no aspect of life is free from government encroachment. A pervasive intolerance for individual rights is shown by government's arbitrary intrusions into private economic transactions and its disregard for civil liberties. And while freedom around the globe has notably increased in the past several decades, many countries have moved in the opposite direction, and most governments still do not respect or safeguard the wide range of civil and economic liberties.

To address those issues, the Cato Institute undertakes an extensive publications program on the complete spectrum of policy issues. Books, monographs, and shorter studies are commissioned to examine the federal budget, Social Security, regulation, military spending, international trade, and myriad other issues. Major policy conferences are held throughout the year, from which papers are published thrice yearly in the *Cato Journal*. The Institute also publishes the quarterly magazine *Regulation*.

In order to maintain its independence, the Cato Institute accepts no government funding. Contributions are received from foundations, corporations, and individuals, and other revenue is generated from the sale of publications. The Institute is a nonprofit, tax-exempt, educational foundation under Section 501(c)3 of the Internal Revenue Code.